# Praise

## Honoring the Mystery

"I recommend *Honoring the Mystery* to anyone who wants to gain greater insight into the expanding inner world of the dying, and particularly to health professionals as they implement a 'person-centered' holistic approach to care. This book is a valuable addition to the literature about people's transcendent experiences in the 'peri-mortal' period – not only those of the dying but also of their families. Knowledge of these well-documented phenomena is relevant for all of us, whether young or old, physically well or close to death. In addition to providing still more evidence that, for the 'Real Me,' death is a transition and not THE END, *Honoring the Mystery* emphasizes the importance of active, empathic listening to enable us to better support loved ones, friends, and patients as they move towards and through the moment of physical death.

As Barbara says, 'In the silence alone, when love is present, profound transformations happen. To listen without judgement, giving space to all that is occurring, may be the greatest gift anyone can give to another human being.'

Let all who have ears to hear, let them hear—but read the book first."

**Dr. Robert Twycross**, *UK Hospice Pioneer and Emeritus Clinical Reader in Palliative Medicine, Oxford University*

"In the midst of apparent confusion in our culture about the nature of death, hospice workers like Barbara Morningstar, who has spent over twenty years working with the dying, can offer some important answers. In this poetic and beautiful recounting of some of her more profound experiences, it is clear that we have nothing to fear about death, and that the lessons gleaned from that extraordinary boundary are most important for the gifts they offer about living a more complete and satisfying life."

**Eben Alexander**, *MD, Neurosurgeon and Author of* Living in a Mindful Universe *and* Proof of Heaven

"I loved reading this beautiful and valuable book. In the hospice where I work, we have a little booklet called, 'Signs and Symptoms of Approaching Death.' We offer this to families who are holding vigil with their loved ones in their final days and hours. It gives information to explain the physical process that is being witnessed in a simple way that lessens fear and brings reassurance.

From now on, I will be strongly recommending Barbara Morningstar's *Honoring the Mystery* as a companion volume. In language that is clear and deeply respectful, Morningstar shares stories and insights from her professional and personal experience that illuminate aspects of the inner journey the dying individual is making, and offers gentle guidance on how to respond with kindness and in a way that will bring encouragement and healing."

*Dr. Michael Kearney is a physician specializing in hospice and palliative care medicine. Originally from Ireland, he now lives and practices in Santa Barbara, California. Additional information about Michael Kearney and his publications can be found at www.michaelkearneymd.com*

"Barbara Morningstar's *Honoring the Mystery* weaves together the many threads connected to end-of-life experiences and the transpersonal dimension of death and dying. Morningstar writes with elegance, clarity, and humility about the remarkable realm that exists at the threshold and awaits those whose eyes and hearts remain open. This is a volume I will surely share with those who want to know more about the great mystery and are curious about experiences that fall outside medical explanations of end of life.

Thank you, Barbara Morningstar, for such a simply-spun and graceful collection that will illuminate lives and shed light on a topic that still remains shrouded in darkness."

*Lisa Smartt*, MA, Co-founder with Raymond Moody of The Final Words Project; Author Words at the Threshold

"Barbara Morningstar is a beautiful writer. Barbara uses story to share a glimpse into the lives of those who are dying and those who care for them. Sacred space is shared and the reader is invited into experiences that enrich life and open doors to questions about life and the transition that we often call death.

For those who have cared for individuals who are dying, or who work in hospice and palliative care, this book may help you gain further insight into your experiences, and/or will open the door to looking for these sacred moments.

For those who have not journeyed with the dying, this book may open the door to new awareness of the dying experience and increase your comfort in being with people in their dying process."

*Kath Murray*, RN, BSN, MA, FT, www.lifeanddeathmatters.ca

# Honoring the Mystery

## *Uplifting Insights from the Language, Visions, and Dreams of the Dying*

Barbara Morningstar

To my gracious father,
for the incredible example you have been in my life
as mentor, protector, gentleman, and inspiration
in how to keep one's heart open and curious at any age
despite the challenges that life offers.

# Contents

# Introduction

When I was in my late twenties I went to a conference in the States that had a spiritual theme. At one point in the main program, a woman by the name of Hannah did a talk about her work as a volunteer at a hospice residence in Connecticut. I had never heard of hospice before and did not realize it involved working with people who were dying. For the majority of people, death is one of the most feared subjects, but her talk stirred just the opposite: it was calming and intriguing. Hannah spoke of unique moments she had had with her hospice patients when they shared experiences as they transitioned to the end of their lives: experiences like seeing a light in the room "calling" them to follow, a light that she could not see but that the patient longed to join as they neared physical death.

Throughout her presentation, Hannah spoke with tremendous grace and peace. Her words inspired me, and I wondered if I would ever be that comfortable with death and dying. I wished for the opportunity to meet her, but I was in a sea of thousands of seminar attendees, so the chances of that happening were slim to none.

When I arrived back home after my travels I looked up "hospice services" and was surprised to find that there was a hospice society within my own town. Further investigation showed that they offered courses for people interested in volunteering with the dying patients. I was intrigued, but I was not about to dive into hanging around dying people! I was young; *life* was much more interesting.

Leap forward one year and I was back in the States for another conference, this time with my new partner, Gordon, who would eventually become my husband. The seminar was hosted by the same group and highlighted spiritual exploration. To my surprise, Gordon actually knew Hannah and her husband! I had the opportunity to meet her and I told

Gordon she had inspired me with her stories about the hospice patients just months before.

What were the chances of that orchestrated meeting?

In the days ahead, I had the privilege of spending time with Hannah and she was the first to encourage me to get involved with hospice work. At the time, I had no idea it would become a career path. This was the first of many orchestrated moments inviting me to get more involved in this profound and sacred work.

Since the moment I began working in the hospice field over twenty years ago, I have been fascinated by the less tangible experiences of the dying and bereaved, those types of occurrences that cannot easily be defined. Rather than defining them, some would say they fall into the realm of mystery. This book is a compilation of such unexplainable stories. The names of the individuals have been changed to protect their privacy. In my personal and professional life I have been blessed with such experiences and have kept dream journals for over thirty years in which I documented my nightly dreams and some personal transformative moments from my time working in end-of-life care. Dreams have been an invaluable source of insight for me and have helped me transition through and heal some of the more challenging losses in my life. In chapter six, I discuss the importance of acknowledging dream experiences for both the dying and the bereaved.

In 2007 when I held the position of program director for a hospice society, I developed a workshop titled "Honoring the Mystery at the End of Life." It was accepted at the British Columbia Hospice Palliative Care Conference as part of that year's regular conference venue. My poster presentation on the same theme was also accepted and placed outside the room where palliative doctors gathered for a week-long workshop series on various elements of end-of-life medical care. For the conference organizers to highlight the poster in that location to be viewed by the doctors was an accomplishment in itself.

Most of the workshops within the conference venue had an average of fifteen to thirty in attendance. My workshop was so popular that despite the fact I was not a keynote speaker at the time, they put me in the ballroom to accommodate the interest. I heard that the final head count was approximately 150 people. This was clearly an unexpected response to my invitation to explore the often-taboo subject of the transcendent experiences of the dying within the medical community. It highlighted a greater need for the discussion to be brought into the open.

At one point during the presentation I had the audience members turn to each other and share mystical experiences that were special to them or that they may never have shared. The room instantly came alive with passionate storytelling. Nurses, doctors, hospice volunteers, social workers, counselors, and spiritual care staff were just a sampling of the participants. When the small-group discussions finished, I invited individuals to share a few of their unique stories with the group as a whole. We celebrated beautiful moments from people's personal lives and their professional careers. Many of those in attendance approached me after the presentation and said it was affirming and inspiring.

I wondered, "Why in the world have we not allowed ourselves a greater opportunity to explore and share these transcendent experiences?"

After that conference I received many invitations from all over the province to present the same workshop to medical personnel working within end-of-life care, to members of hospice societies, and at public venues hosted by hospice and palliative care organizations. The workshop was also accepted for presentation at the Canadian Hospice Palliative Care Conference in Ottawa in 2010. The room was packed, with standing room only at the back—again, a testament to the interest in the subject.

The results were the same: people shared personal stories upon personal stories and we celebrated the theme. Many told me after that they had never had the courage to talk about their experience prior to the workshop. It enhanced my passion and curiosity about the subject matter and in turn deepened my desire to open the dialogue to a greater extent within the medical arena and with the public as a whole.

A friend and colleague who is a respected palliative doctor challenged me one day as I began preparing the material for this book. He was supportive of my writing but asked, "Why is it so important for these stories to exist? I understand and respect that the living need to feel connected to something at the time of dying and after death. But why does it need to be explained? What if we die … the end! Is that so bad?"

I sat with that question for a while.

The truth is these less tangible experiences *can't* be explained fully and it would be foolish to try. They go far beyond a literal context, but I feel it is important to acknowledge, openly discuss, and support the processing of such experiences. Some believe in and share with us the prospect of something more beyond this physical realm; others do not. That is part of the beauty and gift of our unique tapestries and perceptions of life.

My greater response to my colleague was that these stories are really about *life* and its many dimensions, then I went on to share with him some of the profound experiences I had that fall into the realm of mystery, when my own husband died of cancer and within my hospice work. So many of us in our society today push and push and push, always on the go; but, in the interim, how much are we really missing? Not seeing? Not taking the time to discover?

How fully do we really embrace all of life? Why does it often take the challenge of facing physical death to cause individuals to slow down and listen to life in a different way?

Come with me and let us now go together on an adventure of discovery through stories from the dying, from the bereaved, and from my own personal life and my professional career in the hospice field.

# Chapter One

# Adopting the Attitude of an Explorer

*One doesn't discover new lands without consenting to lose sight,*
*for a very long time, of the shore.*
Andre Gide

## Adventurers

Historically we have applauded the courage of explorers who venture into unknown realms. Yet, sadly, the mystery of death—one of the most uncharted realms—is generally not talked about. Many will only speak of it secretly with those who can be trusted not to judge or invalidate a unique event that may have occurred around the time a loved one passed. Though conversations have become more open in recent years, I still find most people are very cautious before sharing any of the less tangible experiences around death with others.

When astronauts went to the moon for the first time, we all waited patiently as they observed with fresh eyes the new territory they were seeing and experiencing. I can still remember waiting up as a child with great anticipation and excitement to watch the moment Neil Armstrong set foot on the moon for the first time. The astronauts did the best they could to describe what they saw. Back in Houston, ground control staff was not ridiculing the space explorers' descriptions. Instead, they were documenting all their reports in order to learn about the new vista these explorers were experiencing.

The same occurred when Christopher Columbus first discovered new land: he carefully documented all his observations to share them with those who awaited his ship's return. All along the voyage, Columbus and his crew were eager to report many new discoveries of land, food, and cultures that people at home never knew existed. These kinds of experiences were not easy to explain to those left behind, who had not taken such a journey, yet they were treated as invaluable new pieces of information to learn from. World views changed as a result of these explorations.

The dying are also adventurers—true explorers venturing into one of the most uncharted territories yet to be discovered. The question is: *Do we honestly listen to what the dying are trying to share or are we too quick to reduce all that they are experiencing by attributing their firsthand accounts to medication, hallucination, or delusion?* At times medications do cause alterations in perception, but sadly all too often, precious experiences that emerge from lucid places are not recognized. They are discounted or overlooked as unimportant, often because they do not fit into a literal category. This can be frustrating for those facing the end of their physical life when attempting to communicate an experience that is less easily defined.

How much are we missing because we have formed concrete opinions about what is possible? What if, along with the dying, the living adopted the attitude of an explorer? What if we listened to what the dying are saying with a different point of view and gave credence to all the unique information they report? Are they giving insight into an experience beyond the physical life we can see?

Palliative medicine is focused on pain management, comfort, and dignity for people dealing with a terminal diagnosis. One of the palliative care doctors I know, who is a very open and cherished colleague, once said to me, "My patients are my gurus."

I found these to be truly wise words.

# A Pair of Lead Boots

While working on the palliative unit at our local hospital in the nineties, I came to know Tom, a young man who was dying of AIDS. At that time, the advanced treatments we have now for this disease were still being developed. Sadly, his partner died three months later of the same illness; they were both very kind and caring men.

Tom and I formed a close bond over the weeks he was with us, but slowly his weight had dropped. Now, emaciated, he was so frail that only a thin layer of skin seemed to cover his skeletal structure.

One day as I walked with him in the hallway, he lost his balance. Concerned that he might fall, I quickly put my arm around his waist to steady him. Immediately, I felt his frailty. My heart broke at the protrusion of his bones under my hands. It was the first time I had held someone who was that weak from illness.

Tom's vulnerability moved me, and I tried to be tender, holding him gently as we continued walking. With great patience I waited for and supported each labored step. Although his energy was compromised, he inspired me with his determination to complete the task at hand. I stayed close and steadied him as we did a brief tour of the unit. It was obvious that he wanted to embrace every last moment of his life.

Only a week later, as I entered Tom's room, I could see that he had taken a dramatic turn. His energy had totally shifted. No longer able to get out of bed, he sat propped up with pillows behind him. Tom watched as I gently sat on the edge of his bed. We were alone in the room and that allowed us greater privacy.

Because those nearing the end of their life become much more sensitive, I adapted my rhythm to his so as not to overwhelm him. We began talking quietly, although Tom had very little life force left. I wondered if it would be easier for

7

him to sit in silence, but then he seemed to want to engage. In the middle of our conversation, he transformed into what I call the Raggedy Ann doll look—his head drooped down, he stared blankly into space, his eyes were wide, and his mouth had opened. I had only seen this vacant look a few times at that point in my hospice work, and I felt somewhat uncomfortable. So I sat in silence and quietly observed him.

Most of us are conditioned by television and movies to think that when people are dying, their eyes and mouth close neatly. But that is not always the case. When a person's eyes remain open in a blank stare, it can be initially haunting for someone to witness. If you wave your hand in front of the person, there is no engaged response. The vacant look stirs concerns that death is near.

Now I found myself sitting on the bed with Tom in front of me, appearing weak and with expressionless eyes. I sat with him in silence and patiently waited, holding my heart open to him with compassion. To bring myself fully into the moment at hand, I settled my mind and breathed into the warmth of my heart. At first, I wondered if he had died in front of me. Nothing is more sacred than being present when a last breath is taken. Would I need to alert the nurse of his passing? But when I took a closer look I could see that Tom was still breathing, if ever so slightly. I felt somewhat relieved but sensed his time here wouldn't be long. After a few minutes passed, Tom suddenly became animated again, as if he had anchored back into his body.

For me, the experience was like watching someone startle awake from a deep sleep and then try to reorient himself to his surroundings. The glow in Tom's eyes returned, and his body moved. At first he seemed a bit surprised to see me and then he turned, scanning around the room to anchor himself. I smiled, and we began talking again. I kept my tone tender and compassionate to match his weakening state.

However, it wasn't long before—once again in the middle of our conversation—Tom's head dropped and the vacant stare returned. His body again appeared lifeless; his eyes were wide open and empty. For the second time in only a few minutes, I held my energy and love carefully around him. It was an intimate moment in the silence, honoring his changing, frail physical presence. Not long after, startled by the change in awareness, he came back to life and reengaged. We began talking softly to each other again.

I had never seen someone go in and out of being conscious mid-conversation before. I was learning to dance with Tom's shifting engagement and I found it touching to be a part of the experience.

Within the span of ten minutes, Tom's "disappearance" happened several times.

Finally, I felt the need to say something to him about it, yet I wanted to remain respectful and in alignment with his beliefs. During our time together over the weeks I had known him, we had established a good rapport. He had told me he believed in life after death; he believed there is something more.

I wouldn't normally have said what I am about to share, but I knew Tom had a good sense of humor. So when he reengaged for the final time during my visit, I jokingly said, "We are going to need a pair of lead boots to keep you in that body!"

He instantly apologized. I laughed and said, "Are you kidding me? If I were you, I would be off exploring the heavens, or doing whatever it is you are doing. I am sure it is much more interesting than talking to me!"

Tom grew quiet and despite the fact that we were alone in the room, he took a moment to look around and out into the hall, as if making sure no one would overhear what he was about to say. Looking directly at me, he whispered, "People used to tell me that 'I' could be in one place while my body was in another, but I didn't believe it until now."

"Well, I believe that can be true," I said. Continuing to gently smile at him, I felt moved by his level of trust. His confiding in me showed that he knew I wouldn't judge him.

Tom winked at me, smiled, and said, "Good, that makes two of us!"

We continued our visit with a playful moment and affirmed each other's perceptions about the reality of both the spirit and the physical body. After a few minutes more, I could tell he needed rest, so I left his room.

Later, I wondered what Tom had been seeing and experiencing beyond the sense of there being something *other* than his body. I wished I could have asked more questions, but to do so would have felt intrusive. I didn't want to impose upon or take away from what he was authentically experiencing.

That visit with Tom turned out to be the last time I saw him. He died within forty-eight hours. I have never forgotten our exchange—what he shared transformed and moved me. In those moments he gave a hint of what he was experiencing beyond his weakened physical shell.

Sitting with Tom in that moment was like witnessing a butterfly gently moving in and out of its cocoon, in anticipation of a departure into undefined territory. Tom's preview of leaving his body behind during the transitional time of dying made me feel as if there is so little any of us really know and understand about death. How can we try to define what is taking place? What are the dimensions beyond the surface of what we perceive to be the truth?

How we hold end-of-life conversations at the turning point of death is of the utmost importance. When we listen to a dying person with grace and a willingness to hear, we open ourselves to learning new things in these interactions. We have so much still to discover from all that the dying share.

This is also beneficial when the bereaved face their time of mourning after a loved one's death. When we, as individuals, can find the courage to explore and listen without judgment, we also support the family members to have a richer experience with their loved one, and this in turn can help with the grieving process. The bereaved often claim to have unique dreams and other types of experiences with the loved one after that person has died. Validating these types of experiences as a normal occurrence is also helpful in the healing process and in coming to terms with the loss.

## Parallels Between the Beginning and the End of Life

As part of people's attempts to understand the dimensions of death, it is not unusual to find parallels between the birth of a baby and the end-of-life transition. The similarities are fascinating in many ways. There are midwives for the expectant mother, and hospice and palliative care workers have been termed midwives for the dying.

When first birthed, newborn babies are in a fetal position similar to when they were cocooned in the womb, adorable little bundles of energy adjusting to their new life. As an individual starts to near the end of their physical life, their capacity for eating, drinking, and socializing declines and they too start to cocoon inward, retreating into longer periods of sleep. This results in less conversation with loved ones as the available life force declines. The dying patient also moves into a form of labor similar to that of a mother during birth. When death draws near, the breath changes in tone and rhythm, indicating the process has begun. In both circumstances, the labor can be easy or it can be challenged and prolonged. Either way, it is essential for the transition at hand.

Individuals facing the end of life also share mystical experiences that are similar to those of children. Young children are more open to their intuitive nature and naturally share their inner experiences. They have not yet been conditioned by society to shut down spontaneous perceptions. Children can have heightened dreams and nightmares. For the dying, mornings and evenings are generally more sensitive as they transition from sleeping and dreaming to awakening.

A person nearing death may talk about seeing people or pets they know that have died. Some children speak of invisible friends. Sadly, if the adults around them are not sensitive enough, the grownups quickly reduce the child's experiences to an overactive imagination and discount their silent playmate or perceptive insights.

As the dying body enters its final stages of breaking down, the person can become more sensitive overall and we can see a resurfacing of the childlike, intuitive nature coming forward more fully again. The dying person may refer to individuals in the room that others cannot see, but who seem real and important to them. Instead of exploring what the person is experiencing, too frequently medical personnel and those closest to the dying person are quick to reduce invisible visitors to delusion or hallucination.

Young children and the dying are both engaged in significant, profound, and what appear on some level to be parallel types of pivotal turning points. Being open to learn from them is key.

## Who Are the Children?

A hospice nurse shared with me an amazing story about the parallel sensitivities of young children and the dying to the less tangible dimensions of life. She told me of a patient in her mid-forties, Diane, who had died of cancer in their hospice residence years before. It had been a challenging time for Diane, with physical and emotional discomfort at home prior to her being admitted. Once in hospice, many of her fears began to settle as she came to know and trust the staff.

She was married with an eight-year-old daughter, Sarah. Her husband was incredibly devoted, spending many hours at her bedside offering his love and support. For Diane, the thought of having to leave them behind was beyond challenging to her heart. One can only imagine how

devastating that would be. Gently, in time,
greater acceptance with the truth of her own m

One particular day when one of the nurses
Diane spontaneously mentioned she could se
running around and asked the nurse who they
could not see the children and shared that with Diane, but she
stayed open to support her patient's experience, watched her
expressions, and asked her to share more about the little ones.
Dianne was lucid as she shared her perceptions, but surprised
and a bit disappointed that the nurse could not see them,
because they were so vivid and alive in her view. She shared
that the children's energy was playful and full of joy; they
made her smile.

Over the next few days, Diane mentioned seeing the joyful
children numerous times. Each time, Diane would ask the
nurse on duty if she too could see the little children, but each
staff member had to admit they were not able to see them.
Even so, staff remained open and gracious in supporting their
patient's experience. Eventually Diane became quiet on the
subject, but she was grateful for the joy they brought to her
heart.

A few days later, Sarah visited her mother Diane in her
hospice room. She hopped on the bed to cuddle close. At one
point during their special visit, Sarah looked over toward the
window in the room and instantly asked her mother, "Who are
those children, Mom?"

Diane was initially surprised but then quickly said, "You
can see the children?"

"Yes," her daughter replied instantly. Sarah could not only
see the children but could speak with them.

Diane told her to ask the children who they were.

After Sarah posed the question to the little ones, she turned
to her mother and said, "They say they are my siblings, Mom,
but I don't know what that means."

.ane then explained to her that it meant they were her ȷthers and sisters. That seemed somewhat confusing, ȷecause Sarah was her only child.

Diane then asked Sarah to ask the children their names. As the children told Sarah their names, she shared them with her mother. It was a deeply moving moment for Diane, as she had had numerous miscarriages in the early part of her marriage and such losses had been very difficult. To deal with her grief, Diane had quietly and privately given a name to each baby she had lost. She had not even told her husband of this soothing ritual. As Sarah shared the children's responses, Diane was amazed that the names matched those she had given to the babies who had not survived to full term.

It was a deeply touching and powerful moment for Diane. Tears welled up in her eyes. Not only had Sarah validated that there were indeed beautiful young children in spirit around her mother's bed, but they were the ones she had felt a connection to as a mother, despite having lost them through miscarriages.

The experience was healing for Diane on so many levels; Sarah had given her a tremendous gift.

The nurse I know was not present when Sarah saw the other children in the room, but she did have the opportunity to sit with Diane after the event. She told me that Diane was comforted in knowing the children were around her. It was soothing and helped her feel she would not be alone in the journey ahead to the end of her physical life and beyond.

Sarah and Diane's shared experience celebrates the parallels between the perceptions of young children and those nearing the end of their physical life.

# Chapter Two

# Metaphoric Language

*Symbolism is the language of the Mysteries...*
*By symbols men have ever sought to communicate to each other*
*those thoughts which transcend the limitations of language.*
Manly P. Hall

## The Beauty of Poetic Exchange

Society teaches us to communicate in literal terms; rarely is the importance of metaphoric or symbolic language discussed. Yet metaphoric language spontaneously surfaces more frequently in communication as people near death. Linguist Lisa Smartt explores this reality in greater detail in her recent book *Words at the Threshold: What We Say as We're Nearing Death.*

As loved ones and caregivers interact with patients, it helps immeasurably when they attune to the symbolic and poetic aspects of the dying experience and listen with a more open set of ears. It is not unusual for topics related to travel and change to be expressed in a more pronounced way during end-of-life conversations. Reflections can surface from the palliative patient such as "Is my passport ready? Has the plane arrived?" This can be a common style of questioning that is not related to any concrete event happening in the patient's outer life; instead, it indicates that at some level they are aware that they will be leaving soon.

Metaphors are often unique to the individual, and if caregivers don't know the person intimately, they may miss what the patient is trying to communicate.

# The Infant's Needs

A palliative doctor shared a story with me about a female hospice patient. Although she was in her nineties, the female patient started referring to her "baby" just weeks before her death. Though she did not have an infant child physically around her, she said that the baby needed her attention but that she couldn't go to the infant at that time. As the weeks unfolded, the baby became a focal point of her conversation and energy. At times, talking about the baby caused her great distress.

The doctor and team were doing everything they could to help the elderly woman with what they initially thought was a symbol with meaning to the patient rather than a reference to something real, but they couldn't decipher what she was specifically trying to communicate. To help the woman attend to "her baby," they even gave her a toy doll, thinking it would help settle her frustration. She was, however, adamant in telling them that the toy wasn't her baby, and she rejected their gift.

At first, no family member, including her husband, knew what the woman was referring to when she spoke about the baby. The doctor asked if there was a real-life experience that might have paralleled her processing and distress. Eventually, the husband remembered that the woman had lost a baby in her teen years. No other family member had been told of the pregnancy, as it was quite controversial at the time. The team then realized their patient was referring to this deceased baby. As the weeks progressed and the woman became increasingly frail, she said she was ready to go to the baby and soon after, she died peacefully.

The patient's bond with her baby became a significant part of her end-of-life language. It was an interesting lesson for the whole team to listen with a different set of ears and realize that her communication revealed a reflective element from her overall life journey in her preparation before departure.

Metaphoric language can often use references such as "wanting to go home," perhaps referring to an otherworldly home. This language is often a telling sign that the person is focused on preparing for the less visible, mysterious transition at hand.

Similarly, a different woman once shared with me that while she was companioning her husband during an emergency room visit, he started quoting a verse from the children's story *Alice in Wonderland.* In the story, Alice ventures through the looking glass into a different and magical world. He repeated the verse from a specific segment of the children's story numerous times with anxious determination until his wife understood that through the metaphor of the story, he was trying to say he would soon die, despite the fact that the doctor had given him a healthy, longer prognosis. The man's metaphoric communication proved to be a premonition, and he died within days of sharing the verse. His death had not been expected as soon, according to the medical staff's prognosis.

Later, his wife said that his sharing of the verse with such determination comforted her with the realization that her husband knew he was leaving and was trying to tell her not to worry. It was his way of saying a final goodbye.

## Kindling in the House

One of the most beautiful examples of symbolic language happened when I was doing a home visit to assess the needs of a family that was trying to support their loved one's desire to have a home death. It still brings tears to my eyes when I reflect on how the conversation unfolded with the patient's wife and their adult children. The love and connection in the family was strong.

Richard was dying of cancer. He had held a leadership role and was well respected in the community for his integrity and passion to serve. He was an intelligent man and clearly the patriarch of the family. When his wife called for hospice support, he was in the final weeks of life.

My conversation began in the living room of their spacious home. The soft light of the sun streamed in the big picture window as we sat on the couches together and shared a warm cup of tea. Richard was weak and was asleep in the other room while we talked. His wife shared the challenges of coming to terms with his death and how the family was working hard to make it a peaceful transition. Their goal was to support his wish to die at home.

There were times he seemed restless and his wife said that his communication made no sense. I asked her to elaborate on some of the things that he talked about and, as we explored his words, I mentioned that sometimes when individuals near death their language becomes much more poetic or metaphoric in nature. In turn, I encouraged her to listen to the words in a different way, since it can make all the difference in exchange. I suggested she read the book *Final Gifts: Understanding the Special Awareness, Needs, and Communications of the Dying*, written by two hospice nurses, Maggie Callanan and Patricia Kelley. They speak of the term "nearing death awareness." The wife then said she would try to obtain a copy to read.

As I was encouraging her to engage with him in this different way, her adult daughter walked in the room, sat on the couch, and joined the conversation.

The daughter loved her father deeply and instantly shared a moment with us, a moment that had happened just days before, when he was questioning her with anxious concern. "Is everyone above ground? Is everyone above ground?" he said. She wasn't sure why he was so insistent on hearing an answer that was affirming.

She then shared with us that if she held his words with a more metaphoric interpretation of the dialogue, she was instantly brought back to a time when the family went scuba diving together. As each member surfaced from the water after the dive, they needed to be accounted for. The final clearance for safety was the question "Is everyone above ground?" When the answer was a clear "Yes," all could breathe a sigh of relief, knowing that each family member was accounted for and safe.

The family then reflected on the fact that perhaps Richard actually needed to be reassured that everyone was okay. Holding his language in a more metaphoric stance resulted in a whole different meaning to his communication.

The son had wandered into the room as the conversation was unfolding. He was very intelligent, and literal outcomes and language were obviously more comfortable for him. As he listened to the reflections we were sharing, he said they initially seemed somewhat far-fetched. However, he then reflected that when he was with his father in a recent intimate moment, Richard looked him in the eyes and asked, "Did you bring the kindling in the house? Did you bring the kindling in the house?" As with the daughter's exchange, the son said there seemed to be a sense of urgency and determination from his father to hear an affirmative answer.

The son said with great skepticism, "That can't mean anything!"

There was silence for the longest time. Then the mother replied, "Well actually, it does mean something, dear. Just after the war, some close friends of ours lived in a remote area in the country. Each year before harsh winter weather came, the husband cut kindling and brought it into the house so they would have enough fuel to keep the fire going and in turn keep everyone warm in the home. This was vital during the cold winter months."

A sudden hush overcame the family as they realized that both metaphors reflected Richard's concerns for the well-being of his precious intimate family members. Did he need to be reassured that they would be all right before he died?

The family then speculated on this prospect. He was loved and respected as the head of the family. Together they decided that if the opportunity arose again they would reassure him they would be okay after he was gone and they would look after each other. It was a touching moment with all of them.

I checked with the family as the weeks unfolded and they told me that though there were times his language was somewhat confusing to follow, more often when they followed the metaphors in a different way, the communication was easier, revealing, and quite profound in its sharing. They were grateful for our conversation and felt it had enriched their time with Richard. They would have missed so much in the exchange if they had ignored his language and not blended with its changing poetic rhythms.

Richard died peacefully at home with his family present. He was reassured that they would be safe, accounted for, and warm in the winter months of grief and mourning ahead.

## The Trip to Disneyland

Art can be a creative way to explore end-of-life needs and the metaphors that accompany them. Often facilitators will use music, crafts, and sand-tray exercises to explore the deeper emotional issues in children's support groups for end-of-life concerns. The heart has a different opportunity to express its needs through these artistic endeavors.

Sylvie had been admitted to a hospice specifically designed to support children (from birth to nineteen years of age) as they faced the end of their physical lives. She was under twelve years old, and her physical body was clearly failing from the ravages of her illness. The hospice is a beautiful facility and the staff is well versed in support not only for the patient but for the needs of parents, siblings, relatives, and close friends.

As the days progressed, Sylvie became weaker and the hospice staff could see she was moving into the final stages of her life. They asked her if there was anything else she would like to do. They wanted to make sure her final needs and wishes were being met. To their surprise she said she wanted to go to Disneyland! At that point in her health trajectory, it was clear the child was too ill to travel. They wondered how best to support this request and decided to give her some paper and writing tools to give her the opportunity to draw and show them what she would need for the trip. The first thing she did was draw a picture of a plane. This was important for the journey. How could she get to Disneyland without that?

The staff was wonderful and continued to support a greater exploration of what else would be needed as she prepared for her travels. As she expressed each request, they would either bring the item to her or work to resolve the concern. Sylvie would then draw the image of that wish in the body of the plane to show that it had been attended to.

When the final request was fulfilled, she created a symbolic image on the plane and announced she was now ready to go to Disneyland. Within twenty-four hours of completing her picture, the child died. Her trip and the drawing became a touching metaphor for all the family members and staff.

This metaphor of the journey and the need to prepare could have easily been missed. The staff was open and creative in their support. Her drawing of the plane was framed and is now displayed on the wall in the children's hospice. It is a beautiful reminder of the power of listening to the less literal language at the end of a person's life and of how Sylvie was able to fulfill her wish to travel to Disneyland.

## The White Canoe

When I was younger and in the initial stages of hospice work as a volunteer (prior to it becoming my career choice), I was also taking acting classes. I had an agent who would arrange auditions for me for commercials and smaller parts for television and film. It was not unusual for me to go into the city for a scheduled appointment after my shift on the palliative unit.

Marilyn was a patient on our unit in the local hospital. She was very personable, and I had visited her on numerous occasions while in my volunteer role. She seemed to enjoy visiting with the volunteers. One day when I walked into her room, the first words out of her mouth were, "Did you get the part?"

"No," I replied, somewhat discouraged by the latest series of rejections after numerous auditions, but getting used to it at the same time. The true art of acting, I was discovering, was about facing oneself: the parts we love and the parts we would prefer not to visit. I loved the pure craft and exploration but hated the "marketing" part. Having to do auditions, compete with others, and try to promote myself were not my favorite experiences. "They don't seem to know where to cast me," I said. On some level I am sure my reservations about the industry came through in my performance when auditioning.

Marilyn's face lit up. "I have the perfect part for you!" she said. "I know this wonderful story titled 'The White Canoe.' It would make a great play for the theater. You could play the Native American princess," she said.

"But I am not Native American," I replied.

"Oh, but you could *play* a Native American," she said.

There is no genetic link in my family to that culture that I am aware of, but I do love nature and when I was a child I would spend hours out in the woods or nature settings exploring its beauty. That was an adventure in itself. At one stage in my youth, I purchased a pair of simple moccasins, no beads, just basic pieces of suede that wrapped around my feet. I loved wearing them so much that over time I almost wore the leather through.

Returning to the part she was encouraging me to play in the story, Marilyn continued, "This is a wonderful story. Yes, you would be perfect for the part!" She became excited at the prospect and proceeded to share this touching and very spiritual Native American love story in her own words; I will share it as best I can recall the telling.

*The story begins with a young warrior who is deeply in love with a princess; the bond between them is strong. Sadly, the princess becomes ill and dies. The young warrior is completely devastated and stricken with grief. The emotions he feels are overwhelming.*

*He is paralyzed by her absence from his life and he questions whether he can go on. Then through the advice of the tribal elders, he is told to fast and purify himself in a vigil: to go within. As he immerses himself in this ritual, he leaves his physical body behind and goes on a search in the spirit world for the one he loves so deeply, all the while celebrating the wildlife and the beauty of nature as he travels. Eventually he comes to the shores of a vast lake, and in the distance he can see an island. He knows that is where his journey will take him. A beautiful white canoe then magically appears. He steps into it and embarks on a voyage across the great span of water that lies before him.*

*As he begins to paddle, to his surprise, appearing next to him in the lake is the princess, also in a white canoe. He is overtaken with emotion and joy upon seeing her again; he can hardly contain himself. Her smile and love help to calm him and are a great support on the journey. His heart is filled with love for her.*

*Eventually they arrive at the island and pull their canoes up onto its shore. Many reflections of their lives and the spirit world have occurred along the way. They embrace each other and begin to walk hand in hand on this beautiful island, once again celebrating their love for each other.*

*After a time, the wind begins to blow, and on its currents the warrior hears a voice calling him back to his physical body. The voice tells him that he is not yet done what he is destined to do in this life and he must return. He will become the chief and rule his people with the great wisdom and love that he has now attained on this vision quest.*

*His heart aches; he does not want to go back. Reluctantly he leaves his beloved behind and returns from the spiritual to the physical world, where he once again picks up his physical body. Over the years, he tells many about his journey into the spirit world. Some believe him, some don't, but in his heart he looks forward to the day he will once again be allowed to return to that special place and be with his beloved again.*

I was sitting quietly next to Marilyn, who was nestled in her hospital bed as she told me the story with great enthusiasm. The images and reflections she shared stirred great emotion and rich meaning within my heart. I was touched that she felt comfortable enough to share it. It was a sacred story for her, and after she finished I told her that I thought it was beautiful. Then I said, "It sounded like he had an out-of-body experience."

"Exactly! That is exactly what he had," she exclaimed. "I have had them in my life, too!"

I was surprised by her honesty, to which I replied, "So have I!"

The minute I shared that, the floodgates opened to a deeper conversation. Our discussion explored the prospect that we are something greater than just a physical body—perhaps an energy force, an essence, some might call it a soul. Due to the experiences Marilyn had had in her life, she absolutely believed this to be true. We were both open to the prospect of life after death and curious about the possibilities of something greater than just the physical realities we know.

She became quite animated during the conversation and mentioned she had forgotten about some of the spiritual experiences she had had in her life. The telling of the story, along with the discussion that followed, helped her to revisit them. She also shared that she rarely talked about them because there were few people she felt comfortable sharing them with. Her concern was that they might be judged or discounted.

Despite her severe weight loss and failing physical health, Marilyn still appeared quite vibrant. In fact the doctors felt it would be months before she died. She told me that, due to her longer prognosis, she would be moved to an extended-care facility in the coming days. We were both in great spirits when we said goodbye. She absolutely insisted that I should receive a copy of "The White Canoe." Though she would be leaving our palliative unit and there were no plans for future visits, she said she was determined to track a copy down and somehow get it to me. I was moved by her offer and said that I would like that very much.

As I left that day I felt enriched by the story that she had shared in our conversation. I wished her well in the move and the resulting transition she would face in the coming weeks. I thought it would be the last time I saw her.

To my surprise, when I walked onto the hospital floor a week later, I was told that Marilyn was not only still there but unresponsive and imminently dying. Her health had taken a turn for the worse and she had not been moved to the extended-care facility as originally planned. I couldn't believe it. What had happened? It took me a little time to take in the new information and prepare my heart to visit her in her final moments of life. Taking a deep breath, I walked down the hall to her room and knocked on the door, as there was family present and I did not want to disturb this sacred time.

Two of Marilyn's adult daughters were with her and they welcomed me in the room. One of their children, Marilyn's granddaughter, was also in the room, sitting next to her bed. I was invited to approach her bedside. I could see that Marilyn had completely changed in appearance. Her fuller face was now sunken and shallow, mouth open and eyes closed. She was unconscious and wore an oxygen mask. The rhythm of her breath was changing, becoming more labored. It was clear that it would not be long before she left this world.

While introducing myself to one of Marilyn's daughters, I shared my surprise at her mother's dramatic shift in health.

"Oh, you are Barbara!" was her instant response. "My mother told me that she wanted to thank you for the discussion you had with her. I am not sure what you talked about, but my mother said the conversation was very important to her."

My mind went back to the week before and the stunning symbolism of the white canoe. I realized that conversation had reminded her of some profound spiritual experiences she had had, experiences that caused her to feel aligned with an identity other than that of her physical body. I wondered if it had helped her in her final transition and preparation to let go of her experience here on earth. My heart was open as I stood at her bedside, and I was deeply moved watching each labored breath she struggled to take as her physical death took greater hold. The family was gracious to allow me into this sacred moment with her.

A little while later, we were out in the kitchen area of the palliative ward and I spent time with Marilyn's daughters and granddaughter. It was wonderful to see how they made it comfortable for the young one to be a part of her grandmother's dying process. She couldn't have been more than ten years old and clearly wanted to be there when her grandmother died. She was very attentive at her bedside.

It is rare in North America to see family comfortable enough to include children in such a loving and open way, but it is an important opportunity to teach them not only about death but about life, love, and relationship. Historically, we gave birth at home and died at home; it is natural, and these were accepted parts of life. I knew it would help this young girl to deal more easily with the future deaths of those she would love during her own life journey. It would also help her in her time of grief.

I then asked if the family would mind if I went in to see Marilyn one last time alone. They were supportive of the prospect and I left them to go into Marilyn's room and stand quietly next to her bed. Her eyes were still closed, mouth gaping open, unresponsive, with her breathing supported by an oxygen mask. Leaning in close, I gently cradled her frail face and head in my hands. With a soft whisper in her ear, I said, "Have a glorious adventure." It was a very, very tender moment for me. It was the last time I saw her; she died later that evening.

The conversation we had had the week before was not only special to Marilyn but also one I will always remember. It felt like a privilege that she had waited long enough for me to have the opportunity to express a final goodbye. I was also touched by the fact that though she could no longer speak, her gratitude for the reflections we shared was expressed through her daughter's kind words that day.

When compiling the stories for this book, I actually spoke to some of Marilyn's daughters and they were able to get a copy of the poem the story she told was based upon. The poem's actual title is "The White Stone Canoe" by Mrs. J. C. Yule. A final wish fulfilled.

# Chapter Three
# Visual Experiences

*I will love the light for it shows me the way,*
*yet I will endure the darkness for it shows me the stars.*
Og Mandino

## Deathbed Visions and Light

People nearing the end of physical life may witness a light illuminating the room or *calling* them to follow it. More frequently, dying patients indicate that they see deceased loved ones in the room with them. Family and those accompanying the dying are generally not able to see the visitor, which can initially cause confusion and concern. Light-filled visions of the deceased coming to greet a loved one who is dying are so common that the palliative medical teams that I worked with would often reflect on its importance in medical rounds. Together we would acknowledge the changing awareness and question whether it was an indicator that the time of death was nearing for that particular patient. David Kessler, in his book *Visions, Trips, and Crowded Rooms: Who and What You See Before You Die*, shares many wonderful stories of these occurrences, collected from medical personnel.

For the dying, these visions are generally comforting; they often express joy and a sense of peace after having had such experiences. Normalizing deathbed visions can be helpful, not only to the dying patient but for families as well. Engaging in dialogue with the individual, asking open-ended questions, and celebrating the vision at hand can add to the person's comfort. Sometimes, the prospect that a departed relative is now present eases the pain of the loved ones who will be left behind. They believe that their departing loved one will not be alone on the journey.

Supporting the exploration of these visual experiences around the dying process, without judgment, adds to a deeper communication and often helps reassure the loved ones who are at the bedside.

After-death experiences of an otherworldly nature are also normal occurrences for those grieving a loss, especially when bonds of love between individuals are strong. At first, the bereaved may hesitate to share their visions for fear of judgment; but later, when trust has developed, they often confide in us. Many recently bereaved people tell hospice staff, counselors, and volunteers that while they are awake or during a dream in the sleep state, it is not unusual for them to see their deceased loved one in a recognizable vision or a light-filled form.

Young children and animals are deeply intuitive and often respond without a filter to an invisible presence in the room. When a child shares a vision they are having or claims to see a deceased loved one, parents ask for guidance: they are not sure what to do. It is important to reassure them that this type of visual experience is normal and has been documented throughout history.

## A Mother's Unending Love

Jill was a longtime hospice volunteer in her senior years who had supported many people to the ends of their lives during her time of service. She was loved by volunteers and staff alike, myself included.

One day while I was sitting at one of the little desks in our team room on the palliative unit, preparing for medical rounds, a member of the consult team came over and shared with me the news that Jill was in the hospital and would soon be admitted into the palliative program as a patient. I was shocked and saddened at the news. She had been feeling a little unwell in the previous weeks, but she told us she thought she might just be coming down with a cold. No one would have ventured to predict a palliative diagnosis.

Jill and I had worked together a long time and we were quite close, so I quickly headed down to the medical floor she had been admitted to and ventured into her room to check in. She was grateful to see me. It had been a rough day and what initially was thought to be a nasty flu bug had been diagnosed as an aggressive form of lung cancer. She only had months to live; the palliative doctor had visited her just hours before my visit, gently breaking the news to her about her limited prognosis.

When I got closer to her hospital bed, I could see she was tired; she seemed deep in thought, perhaps still slightly shocked by the news and trying to process all that was being discovered about her health. Yet somehow she also seemed calm. As hard as this news was for Jill, I knew her well and suspected that all the years of hospice work would help her face the journey that was in the process of unfolding. As I sat on her hospital bed, listening to her story as she reflected on hearing the news of her mortality and how she might embrace the weeks ahead, I was moved by her courage. It was clear that she wanted to make this time as meaningful as possible.

At one point, she shared with me that she had had an interesting experience only months before. She said that early one morning, she awoke to see her mother clearly standing at the foot of her bed. Jill was in her eighties and her mother had died close to forty years earlier, so this was a rather startling event at first.

I asked her, "Was it peaceful?"

She responded by telling me that her initial reaction was one of great joy. She loved her mother very much and was excited to have this mystical experience with her. Their love still remained and was present in the experience. All of this was occurring prior to her cancer diagnosis. Then another reflection came over her: as a longtime hospice volunteer, she

was aware of patients' seeing dead loved ones comin
them when they were near death. So her second imp
her mother's visit was one of wonder and slight ᴗᴗ
"Why are you here now?" she thought to herself.

Her mother did not speak during the visit but did bring a tremendous sense of love and peace to Jill in that moment. It was a very special experience for her: clear and lucid and very impactful. She was not on any significant pain medications at the time, which often causes people to dismiss the reality of such visions.

As she reflected on the event with me, she said she now understood why her mother had come. She felt it was to prepare her for the news that her death would be drawing near and to remind her that she would not be alone. Her mother's love and support would be with her in the transition.

The experience had a tremendous impact on Jill, and I felt privileged that she had been comfortable enough to share it with me. It clearly helped her face the news of her own mortality.

As the weeks and months progressed, Jill's health declined and she moved into the last phases of physical life. She naturally started cocooning, becoming quiet but preparing for a different transition and birthing away from this life that we know in a physical sense—a birth into a transition beyond what we can see or fully define. I was able to visit with her many times in the weeks leading up to her death.

One day I was doing some work at my office in our hospice resource center, which was located away from the hospital. As I was sitting at my desk, I got a really strong "nudge" to go to the hospital in that moment. My mind rebelled. I looked at the clock, thinking that I didn't need to leave for another hour, but the impression was clear that I should head there *now!* So I gathered my things and headed off to the hospital early for the regular weekly scheduled palliative medical rounds. When I arrived at the hospital I was also amazed at how quickly I found a parking spot. It was such a busy place that I could drive around for fifteen or twenty minutes sometimes just to find a spot. That day as soon as I pulled into the lot someone pulled out in front of me and I got a parking spot instantly!

Walking into the lobby of the hospital I realized I now had a whole extra hour, and since I hadn't yet eaten I thought I would stop and just quickly pick up a sandwich at the coffee shop in the lobby entrance. As soon as that thought entered my mind, another intuitive "nudge" came through very strongly in the form of an inner command:

"*No*, don't stop for a sandwich; go to the palliative unit now. Go *now!*"

It was as strong and clear as the prompting I had had earlier to go to the hospital.

So I decided against the sandwich and rushed directly to the palliative unit. I knew that Jill had been imminently dying in the days before and I had already said my goodbyes, not knowing if she would be there when I got to the unit for medical rounds that day. When I went up to the nurses' station they told me she was still alive but very close to death. Her daughter, Heather, was with her and the nurses felt my support would be of value because she was struggling with having to say goodbye. I knew Heather through Jill's years of volunteer experience, and as a result I knew how close their bond was. Heading to Jill's room, I quietly entered and offered my support.

Heather was standing at her mother's bedside, holding Jill's hand; she was immersed in deep emotion. Jill was clearly in the final labor pains of dying. She was unresponsive; the rhythm of her breath had changed—it was different in tone and expression. Over the years, I have observed how hard it is for families to experience this transition for the first time, but it is a natural and expected part of the dying process. As far as we know it is not painful, and the palliative team of nurses and doctors do everything they can to make sure the person is comfortable at this time.

I wanted to make sure my presence was welcome at such an intimate moment, so I went over to Heather, gently putting my hand on her shoulder to let her know I was there. As soon as she saw me, the tears began to flow even more. She was grateful I had come and invited me to stay. I wrapped my arms around her in a big, warm hug, freeing her to fully express her emotions. After I held her for a time, she settled, and I went around to the other side of the bed and tenderly took hold of Jill's frail hand. It was limp and warm, but I knew on some level she would be aware of my presence and love. As I wrapped my hand around hers and held it in mine, I made the intention of opening my heart to her as she prepared to leave. I knew it would not be long.

On the other side of Jill's bed, Heather cried and spoke of what had unfolded in the days since I had seen them. It was touching to be reminded of this deep mother-daughter bond. I couldn't have been there more than ten minutes when something rather unique occurred. It is hard to explain in words that fully capture the experience. Though Jill was unresponsive, in the next moment it was as if I could feel her squeeze my hand, not in a physical sense but in a much deeper way, on an intuitive level. It felt like a final squeeze to say goodbye. This caused me to look more directly into her face, and then, instantly, her breathing shifted and she took her last breaths. She had died.

Her daughter was on one side of the hospital bed, holding her hand, and I was on the other.

The change of breath and the last moment can sometimes be so subtle that they are easy to miss. Jill's daughter had been talking while this occurred, and I gently let her know her mother had died. She stopped talking and focused more intently on her mother's face. With a deep breath, she drank in the truth that Jill was gone, and tears again began to flow. We held the sacredness of the moment for a while and then called the nurse into the room to do a formal pronouncement of death.

Jill's daughter looked at me and said, "If there was anyone Mom would have wanted here to support me at this time it would have been you. It is almost like she waited until you got here, so I wouldn't be alone."

I was touched by her comment but also absolutely amazed at the timing and the strong promptings that had encouraged me to go to the hospital earlier than my planned time. If I had waited even ten minutes longer, clearly I would have missed this sacred and intimate moment. I too marveled at the orchestration of events.

It is such a privilege to be invited into the moment when someone dies. This was no exception. I came around the side of the hospital bed and put my arm around my dear colleague's daughter and held her close as the tears flowed. My heart was both sad and full. I would miss Jill, but what a gift to have been there to say a final goodbye. I was thankful for that opportunity.

We stayed together for a while, and then I left Heather to have some final moments alone with her mother. It was a sacred, sacred time indeed.

The timing of someone's death is always interesting to observe. Sometimes loved ones are there and close, and other times it is almost as if the dying person waits to be alone. It is often when the bonds of love are the strongest and the close family member leaves for that ten-minute cup of coffee that the departure takes place. Is it because sometimes it is easier to leave and not have to say goodbye face to face? The bond is so deep that it is harder? We will never fully know, but somehow, love always seems to be at play.

The deeper question is, Are we truly ever alone when such a transition occurs?

# A Welcoming Committee

Myra was one of the very experienced palliative nurses I had the privilege of working with over the years. She has worked in the field for over thirty years and is a very committed and compassionate nurse, always focused on the highest care and well-being of both patient and family.

This story happened in the early part of Myra's career, when she felt a deep calling to work with patients dealing with terminal illness. At the time, she was on staff at a small eight-bed palliative unit at a local Catholic hospital. She had just started the evening shift when she walked into one of her patients' rooms. The patient's daughter, Nancy, was sitting quietly at the bedside of Jane, her frail and failing mother. Myra introduced herself and let Nancy know she would be attending to her mother that evening and would also be present to support Nancy as well. She made the daughter a cup of tea and then they sat together at the mother's bedside.

Nancy then turned to Myra and said, "Mom has been in a coma for the past few days and cannot communicate. When Mom was home there were so many things I wanted to say to her, so many questions left unanswered. But there were too many visitors, so I never got the chance."

Nancy cried softly as Myra embraced and reassured her. Myra also told her that it is believed to be true that hearing is one of the last senses to go, even when a person is unresponsive and nearing death. She encouraged Nancy to continue to share her thoughts and feelings with Jane as if she were still able to respond. Eventually, Myra left Nancy at the bedside alone with her mother for some private time. After spending some time with her mother, Nancy left for home, feeling as though she had had a load lifted from her heart. Myra's supportive encouragement had been invaluable.

Myra carried on with her bedtime care with the other palliative patients on the unit. Later she returned to Jane's room to check in on her. As she approached the bedside, Myra

ɔduced herself by name, even though Jane was
e, and let her know she would be her nurse for the
ould make sure she was comfortable. She then
her, but while Myra fluffed the pillows, Jane
...ᵖᵉᶜᵗᵉdly opened her eyes as wide as saucers, stating, "I
am ready to answer the questions!"

Myra was completely taken aback, since she was not
expecting her to suddenly become alert and awake. She had
been comatose for the previous two to three days, so this was
quite a surprise.

Myra repeated Jane's statement as a question: "You are
ready to answer the questions?"

Jane replied, "Yes, I am ready to answer the questions."
With that she sat straight up in bed, supporting herself with
Myra's arms wrapped around her, and proceeded to exclaim
with great excitement, "Glory, glory, hallelujah! There they
are!"

When Myra's nursing partner arrived in the room, she was
completely surprised by the sight she witnessed. She rushed
off to get the husband's phone number and call the family
back to the hospital. Myra described the patient as having an
"illuminating aura" about her as they shared this mysterious
event at the end of her life. Jane continued gazing blankly into
the distance with great joy, crying out, "Glory, glory,
hallelujah! There they all are; they are calling me to come!"

Myra held her close and told her that if they were waiting,
she should go.

Jane then abruptly looked into Myra's eyes and laughingly
said, "I can't go yet!"

She reassured her, "Sure you can."

"I can't. I don't have any clothes on!" She then looked
back toward the familiar "unseen" faces and stated, "I guess
when I was born I didn't have any clothes on either." All the
while she was laughing in such a contented manner.

As Myra continued to cradle Jane's frail body, waiting for
the family to arrive, she asked Jane, "Who is calling you?"

Jane then clearly called out several names, pausing, nodding, and smiling in between each name as if to acknowledge each individual independently. Myra said there was no paper close by, so she reluctantly grabbed the closest pen she could find and quickly scribbled the names on the crisp white hospital bedsheets. It was a Catholic hospital and she wasn't sure how the nuns would feel about that!

Jane's husband, her son, and her daughter Nancy arrived back within minutes. They were visibly shaken and astounded to find their loved one alert and bubbly, wanting to "answer the questions!" The nurse then described how she awoke with enthusiasm and called out a list of names. The family looked through the list and was able to identify each of them as family, friends, and even family pets who had died! It was surprising for all involved that Jane included the family pets that had died in previous years as part of the group coming to greet her with the other loved ones.

Myra said the "awakening" lasted until about 3:00 a.m., when Jane then gently lapsed back into a coma after answering the family's questions and saying her goodbyes. She died peacefully two or three days later.

Such experiences can occur regardless of belief; it does not seem to matter whether the person is religious or spiritual or atheistic or agnostic. Myra said the woman wasn't a particularly religious person, but the experience she shared before leaving helped to comfort the family members. It was also a comfort to Myra as both a nurse and a human being; it has inspired her in her work as a palliative nurse over the years since.

## The Rainbow

Many years ago, in my initial days of hospice work, I was assigned to support an elderly couple who had been married for over fifty years. Their partnership was strong, but the husband had been ill with cancer for a number of years. The illness was clearly now taking greater hold and moving him closer to the end of his physical life. His wife was doing everything possible to keep him at home, but as he became weaker this was becoming more and more challenging. He had been in and out of the hospital in the preceding weeks, needing blood transfusions more frequently, and his elderly wife was becoming more exhausted by the demands of attending to his round-the-clock care.

During my shift on the palliative care unit, while visiting many of the patients and their families, I heard that the man had just been brought in by ambulance with his loyal wife at his side. The other family members were on holiday out of town at the time, and she had been attempting to manage on her own. The couple had come to the hospital because he had taken a turn for the worse and become very weak and unresponsive.

As the nursing staff was settling him into his hospital room, I connected with his wife in the hallway. She was quite distressed, with deep emotions surfacing, wondering if he would pull through and go home again or die in the hospital. She felt she had failed him by bringing him to the hospital, since he had wanted to die at home. I reassured her that she was right to have brought him to the palliative unit and that once he stabilized, we would have a better sense of how things would unfold. She went back in the room to sit with him in silence.

So many times over the years when working with this couple, I had watched this man come close to death and rally. Quietly, inwardly, I whispered, "If you could just show me what will happen, it would help. Will he go home or will he die soon? If I had a sense of which will happen, I could better prepare and be present for the family." Surrendering my internal question, I then went on to check on some of the other patients.

It had been a stormy, windy day. Not more than ten minutes had passed after I asked my question, when the clouds broke and the sun shone through the darkened sky. It streamed into the rooms on the hospital unit. When I walked into this man's room, to my surprise I saw the most stunning sight. Next to his bed was a large picture window, and framed magnificently by the window panes was the most vibrant of rainbows. It was so close, it felt as if I could have reached through the glass window and touched its radiant light. The wife was leaning over her husband at the bedside, and as I stood next to her I placed my hand on her shoulder and gently encouraged her to turn around. As she looked behind, she too was amazed at the light and the rich colors of the rainbow before her. Neither of us had experienced a rainbow so close.

What was even more moving was that when I went to the window to get a closer look, the rainbow was literally touching the roof of the hospital outside this man's window, reaching up into the sky like a big staircase. The staircase metaphor was so strong for me in that moment that my heart just knew he would not return to his physical home, but rather that he would leave this world from his hospital bed. It was also a very tender moment for the couple. I decided to keep my reflection to myself and stood in silence with them, caught up in the breathtaking image before us.

The man had slept through the whole event, and both his wife and I thought the rainbow was so exquisite that we wanted to share it with him. So I went to the foot of his hospital bed and jiggled his big toe, quietly calling his name. He woke up for the first time since his arrival. It took a moment for him to catch his bearings, but then I encouraged him to look out the window. As he turned to look, his face became illuminated by the magnificent sight. I walked over and stood next to the window. He had been a painter in his life, and they were a religious family. I smiled at him, drinking in the beauty, and said, "I think God painted this just for you."

No words were spoken, but he just beamed with joy. His smile was radiant and infectious. Together, we embraced the beauty in silence; it was a sacred moment.

When I later walked out onto the hospital floor, I could see other portions of the rainbow through various windows. It was completely arching over the corner of our palliative unit on the top floor of the hospital. It was a stunning sight and seemed to highlight the unit as a gateway to something greater than what we can see. Not long after, the rainbow slowly faded away.

Weeks passed, and with his usual resilience the man rallied once again. I wondered if I had misinterpreted my sense of the rainbow's reaching into the expanse of sky foretelling his passing. Yet in the moment when it occurred the message had seemed so clear.

One evening not long after, I was on the palliative unit again. When I walked in his room to visit this patient, I found he was alone and sound asleep. He had taken a recent more challenging turn in health and vibrancy. I stood in silence by his bed and happened to notice some inspirational cards that had been sent to him during his hospital stay. One card stood out to me from the rest—on the face of that card was a picture of an arched rainbow. The caption read: "The rainbow, the rainbow, the smile of God is here." It paralleled the experience that had taken place only weeks before, when the rainbow had been touching the roof of the hospital just outside the window of his hospital room. I wondered if his time here would now be drawing closer to an end.

Only a few days passed, and the man died peacefully on the palliative care unit with his family at his side, as was foretold by the stunning image of the rainbow weeks before. The radiance and light of the rainbow touched us all in profound and transformative ways the day it manifested, providing comfort for the patient and those eventually left behind to grieve and heal.

# Chapter Four

# Auditory Experiences

*The earth has its music for those who will listen.*
Reginald Holmes

## The Sublime Sounds in Transition

A uditory experiences in the end-of-life transition have not been talked about as frequently as visual images. More recently, Eben Alexander, MD, in *Proof of Heaven* speaks passionately about the music he heard. He says it guided him during his near-death-experience journey.

People share auditory experiences that manifest in a variety of forms. They will speak of hearing a celestial or symbolic sound of music, a deep electrical hum, or sounds of nature such as wind, ocean, and birds, to name a few. Sometimes the sounds will be metaphors for experiences in the person's life. A former railroad conductor, when nearing death, heard the sound of a train whistle, indicating the train's imminent arrival to take him on a journey.

Both the dying and the bereaved will talk about experiences in which they hear the voice of a departed loved one. The voice speaks words of comfort and reassures the listener that even though they have passed on, they are all right. Although it is often surreal for loved ones at the bedside to witness the dying person's experiences in the same way, auditory events with the previously departed are generally comforting for the dying individual.

Sometimes we hear of a deceased person calling for the dying person to join them. On occasion, it can be frustrating for the patient if they are not ready to leave and feel hurried by a voice calling them to follow into the afterlife. However, later, it can comfort the palliative patient (and their loved ones) to know that a loved one who has previously passed or a respected spiritual figure is waiting to accompany them when they are ready to move on.

## Beautiful Music

Janice was a palliative patient in her early fifties. She had been on our palliative unit for a number of weeks for pain management and to receive added treatment to improve her quality of life. This particular day, however, she received the news that unfortunately the cancer had spread to another major organ and was inoperable—not easy news for anyone to hear. It was a tough day, especially because up to that point she had hoped for the possibility of regained health and still held an element of hope for recovering fully.

While I was standing at the nurses' station just after hearing the news myself, a minister came to the front desk and asked for Janice's room number. He was a kind man, and I directed him to her room. Knowing their conversation would take some time, and not wanting to interfere in any way, I went to visit with some of the other patients.

I was walking in the hallway past her room an hour later when I got a little "nudge" to check in and see how she was doing, so I knocked on the door and went in for a visit.

The minister had just left, and Janice was sitting alone in her room, deep in thought on the edge of her bed. The sun was streaming in from the window on the opposite wall, giving gentle light to a challenging time of introspection for her.

In the most tender way I could, I asked how the day was going for her, putting my hand on her shoulder in comfort. She had been on the unit for a number of weeks and we had formed a strong connection. Her roommate of a similar age had died only a few days before, and that bed was now empty—that death had added to her facing her own mortality more clearly. Now the new piece of information was resulting in another tough day for her to process all that was unfolding.

Janice slowly looked up at me, as though a weight was on her shoulders, and said, "I guess if you have faith, God will look after you?"

This was such a probing question, and I could tell by the look in her eyes that she really wondered if faith alone would be enough. Spiritual and religious questioning is a normal occurrence as people move more fully into the realities of dying. Thoughts and feelings can surface that aren't expected; the process of dying is not always what they imagined it to be. "What will this *really* be like now that I am in the midst of the transition?" is a natural and healthy response as the truth of an experience takes greater hold.

It was obvious that the conversation with the minister had caused Janice to reflect a great deal. She asked what I thought about this, and from previous conversations I knew that she believed in life after death. I looked at her and said, "Death can be a celebration for some. Many believe that we never really die, but rather we just move to a whole series of new and exciting experiences in other worlds."

I am always careful when responding to such patients' questions, since I have supported people of so many different religious, spiritual, and cultural backgrounds. This includes many individuals who are also atheistic and agnostic, each to be honored fully for what brings them comfort during this tender turning point. I did, however, feel comfortable to continue with more reflections based on Janice's beliefs, as she had invited me to do so. I then began to describe the experiences that some patients have and that I have witnessed, which are so beautifully termed "nearing death awareness."

I then shared some of the loving and magical moments that I have had with patients over the years when their awareness started to change as they neared physical death. Oft times, patients have shared that they see people in the room that I couldn't see, and I recognized the comfort the presence of that person brought them. I suggested to Janice that she stay open to everything, and to pay attention to her dreams and any unique experiences that might come to her. She instantly replied that she had been having more dreams with her mother recently, even though her mother had passed away a number of years before. They were very comforting to her. They felt real to her.

As we talked, her whole countenance changed. It was as if a weight had been lifted off her shoulders. I was inviting her to be an observant participant in this new adventure in a whole different way. She sat taller in bed, we laughed, and she seemed fascinated with the stories of people's experiences that I was sharing.

She was quiet for a moment, and then she said she had not heard about such experiences before and thought all of what we talked about was really interesting. When I left the room she was in good spirits.

One evening just a few days later, I was in the hospital because one of the other patients was getting very close to dying and I had been called in for extra support. When I was standing at the nurses' station a few of the nurses were discussing the fact that Janice now claimed to hear music! I smiled at the news, but then I was concerned when some of the nurses just assumed she was probably hallucinating due to medication. This is often the first response by most medical personnel.

As I listened to the dialogue I wondered quietly to myself, if I should challenge this conversation or not? I was still in my early years of hospice work and was a little nervous to speak up for fear of being judged myself. Nevertheless, I took a deep breath and said, "Maybe what she is hearing is very real for her."

In that moment my thoughts drifted back to my experience of meeting with Elisabeth Kübler-Ross years before. She was a pioneer in standing up for the rights of the dying. She and I spoke together of similar moments she had witnessed with dying children, and she validated the reality that music was a real part of the experiences they sometimes shared.

Palliative nurses are dedicated and cherished individuals who work hard in a very demanding arena. I was moved when, instead of resisting my statement, they were actually quite receptive, and that led to a discussion about the less tangible experiences of the dying. Were they actually of a spiritual or otherworldly nature? Some of the nurses even thought it would be interesting to have an evening to discuss this topic alone. Obviously they had been privy to many unique experiences themselves, perhaps not always feeling comfortable about how to share them.

Janice was resting that evening, so I did not go and visit her until a few mornings later. As we sat in conversation, the subject turned to the sounds she had been hearing, and I asked her to share more of the experience. She was sitting on the edge of her bed, and her whole face lit up in response. "They are all the hymns I loved as a child. They are so beautiful, nothing like I have heard before, of a different quality that is hard to describe."

I smiled and honored the gift of music she was explaining in greater detail. Together we celebrated what she described as a rich celestial sound. She went on to tell me that the music was playing all the time; she could even hear it in the background when people were talking. When people were in the room, the volume would turn down, and when people left and she was alone, it would turn up again and fill the room. When I asked her how it made her feel, she said it was soothing and comforting. It was a sound that was beyond description and brought her a deep sense of peace. Her countenance had changed dramatically since our last conversation. Her newfound joy was inspiring.

She was so excited that she began to tell all kinds of people about her experience with this beautiful music. She told one of her friends in the church choir, and she said that her friend thought it must be a special gift from God. She even told two different ministers and their wives when they came to visit.

Sadly, instead of celebrating this revelation with her, they seemed to think it a bit unusual; they had never heard of it before. She told me later that she wondered why they didn't know about this; she was a little disappointed in their response.

The music was very real for her, and the beauty of its presence gave Janice the strength she needed to go home and get her affairs in order. She returned to the palliative unit a number of weeks later, even frailer and closer to the end of her life. Though she still faced personal challenges as the illness progressed, she mentioned hearing the heavenly music until the day she died.

## A Husband's Final Gift of Love

During a talk I gave to a hospice society on the mystery of death, Deborah, one of the board members who was present, shared this touching story about an experience she had after her husband died. It moved everyone in the audience to their core, and I am grateful that she has allowed me to include it here.

Dave's initial diagnosis of cancer had surfaced when he was only eighteen. Deborah was made aware of his health history when they met many years later. At the outset they made a decision that love would be their anchor and guide.

Dave died when he was thirty-two, making Deborah a widow at twenty-nine. When they married, they did not know they would be privileged to have just seven years together. The death of a loved one is not an easy experience to traverse at any age, but it seems even more out of the scheme of what we expect of life when it occurs in our younger years. Deborah was struggling with the myriad of emotions that surface during the grieving process. She wanted to get on with her own life again, but her heart also needed time to integrate such a devastating loss.

Deborah had one final day to herself before returning to work. Early that morning, she lay in bed wondering how she would find the strength to reenter the office setting. A part of her was very nervous about the thought, since her husband had died only six weeks before. She was grateful for the support her colleagues had provided during his illness and wondered how they would react when she returned. Ironically, she said she was concerned about being strong for them.

As she reflected on the following workday, Deborah was quite anxious about the prospect of waking up on time, due to the intense journey of grief she had been through in the weeks before. It is not unusual to feel exhausted after a significant death as one traverses the wide range of emotions at play. She managed to pull herself out of bed that morning and decided to make a soothing cup of tea. While she sipped the warm brew, a smile came over her face as she remembered that Dave was notorious for waking up before the alarm went off. He then would gently rub her back and whisper in her ear, "Honey-pie, it's time to wake up." Thirty seconds later the alarm would ring!

She often teased him about the fact that as long as he was in the house they would not need an alarm. Deep emotions surfaced as she reflected on those playful moments. In the midst of her intense grief, Deborah wondered if those memories would one day soothe her rather than stimulate more tears. She continued to prepare for the next day of work.

It was clear by the way she initially shared her story with me that their bond of love was deep and lasting. As she settled into bed that night she lay quietly with her thoughts as the soft light of the moon streamed through the window. She reflected on her belief that love never dies and that it will survive even beyond physical death. She prayed that this was true and asked God to help her. She then whispered to Dave these tender words: "I love you, my darling, and I somehow know you are near. Our love must see us through. It must. Remember it's a forever thing for us." Deborah then quietly drifted off to sleep.

The next thing she remembered was feeling a gentle pressure on her back that felt comforting and warm. A clear voice then whispered in her ear, "Honey-pie, it's time to get up now." Half-awake, she then rose out of bed and walked toward the doorway, spontaneously answering, "Thanks, honey, I'm up." The room was also filled with her husband's fragrance. All of a sudden, she stopped at the doorway, turned around, and looked back at the empty bed. She marveled at what had just taken place. As with their normal routine when Dave was alive, he had woken her up before the alarm went off. Shortly afterwards the alarm actually sounded; the timing added to the unique event.

Deborah was overwhelmed with emotion and elated. She felt that Dave had come back to reassure her that he had survived death and was now in spirit. What a gift to her heart! She had the privilege of feeling his touch, hearing his voice, and breathing in his fragrance one last time. This unexpected moment caused her to both laugh and cry simultaneously.

She truly felt it was real, not her imagination, and it felt like a confirmation of Dave's transition to the spiritual life. The experience made her feel strong, and it was clearly life-changing. Her fear and anxiety also dissipated. She had a renewed energy and enthusiasm to return to work.

When she arrived back at the office, she smiled despite the concern her colleagues were displaying. She shared how happy she was to be back and greeted them with warm hugs. She said it was ironic that her team cried and needed the Kleenex, not her!

The shadow of her grief had been lifted by the beautiful experience with Dave that morning. For her it was a testament to their bond. Her question about the eternal nature of love after a physical death was answered through his familiar loving presence and final act of love to wake her.

# A Grandmother's Love

Chantelle, a wonderful and very compassionate nurse I know, shared a beautiful moment she had with Susan, a young patient in her thirties who spent her last days of life on the palliative unit in the hospital.

Susan was struggling with the ravages of cancer, and it was clearly winning in its dominance over her remaining life force. Her body had become very frail. As her attending nurse, Chantelle had come to know the patient and her family during their stay on the unit. She offered comfort and ease to everyone during Susan's end-of-life transition.

As the days progressed, Susan often found it more comfortable to sit up in one of the easy chairs at her bedside as opposed to lying in the bed. Chantelle knew it would not be long before she left this world.

The patient's mother had been visiting regularly. The loss of a child, no matter what the age, somehow seems out of the expected scheme of life events. It is certainly not easy for a parent to have to say goodbye to one they have birthed.

At one point, Chantelle walked into the patient's room to administer some of the needed pain medications. Susan was propped up in her usual chair and her mother was standing in front of her. As Chantelle was attending to her, Susan spontaneously started singing a song. Her mother was surprised and quickly asked her, "How do you know that song? Only Grandma knew that song."

Susan looked her mother in the eyes and instantly said, "Don't you see? Grandma is standing right there singing!" This was a curious comment because Susan's grandmother had died just a few years earlier. She was not physically present in the room; no one else could see her.

Chantelle said it was a moment she will never forget. The hair on her arms stood straight up with the thought of Susan's grandmother's spirit standing there, but it was coupled with such a rich sense of peace and love. The mother fell silent and tears welled up in her eyes as she took in her daughter's answer—the song Susan had been singing was from the mother's childhood, a song that *her* mother had sung to soothe her. Now the grandmother was singing the same song to support and nurture Susan in the last throes of her physical life. It was also reassuring for the mother not only to once again hear the song but also to know that her mother was there supporting her daughter at such a challenging time. Both were being soothed by the heartfelt melody the deceased grandmother was singing.

Susan died within the next forty-eight hours. Chantelle said it was a powerful moment she will never forget, the words of the song a touching memory.

# Chapter Five

# Kinesthetic Awareness

*Your body is away from me,*
*but there is a window open from my heart to yours.*
Attributed to Rumi

## The Gentle Sense of Presence

When people are dying or grieving, they sometimes speak of feeling the presence of someone near who can't necessarily be seen with our eyes. The dying may claim to feel someone prompting them to take the next steps. More often it is those in grief who share with us a sense of the loved one who has just passed on, now near to them, bringing comfort and reassurance of their love.

People have spoken of the feeling of the wind rushing past in the quiet of a room and having a sense of their loved one wrapping around them, when in fact that person is far away at the hospital imminently dying. How can that occur when they are in different locations? Shortly after the sensation has passed, the phone rings and it is a nurse from the hospital calling to share the news that the person whose presence they just felt has died, confirming the earlier impression of that individual's energy—their essence—really having been with them at the time. Were they perhaps passing through with a final goodbye?

Many have also described feeling the presence of a loved one wrapped in a metaphor that is symbolic of who they are. This can manifest as their favorite song coming on the radio just as the bereaved simultaneously feels the essence of that person around them. Others have said that an image of

51

something that reminds them of the dying person in a symbolic way will appear at the same time as the sensation of the deceased being close at hand. This experience is not frightening, but rather comforting.

## A Protective Hand on My Shoulder

I clearly remember one stormy winter night when I was in my early twenties growing up in Ontario. I was invited to a friend's house to spend the evening with some of her friends. This particular young woman's friends often met at various clubs in town. I never really could tolerate alcohol, so I was not the type of person to frequent the bar scene in my youth. When I arrived, I realized that perhaps I was just a little more introverted than the group at hand. I also quickly realized I did not have a lot in common with these women and got quite restless listening to their conversations. They seemed nice enough, but I just didn't fit in. After a few hours of feeling out of place, I decided I was going to politely thank the host and make a quick exit from the party.

When I went to get up, however, there was a sensation of a hand on my shoulder, as though someone was pushing me down, holding me in my chair. It was strong and felt real. I can still remember the physical impression. At the same time, I had the impression of a voice whispering, "You don't need to leave now. Stay. Just stay a little longer." Though this sensation was strong, I shook it off and went to get up. Again, I felt someone standing beside me, hand hard on my shoulder, holding me in my seat. I decided that if a presence was lovingly encouraging me to stay, the company couldn't really be all that bad!

So I stayed, at least for a while, at least another half hour to forty-five minutes. Soon I again became restless; I'd had enough. The conversation was just not resonating with me and I had things to attend to the next day, so I stood up and said goodbye. This time, there was no hand on my shoulder, no sense that someone was standing there encouraging me to stay. This time, I was free to go.

As I was driving home, I could see the freeway had become very slippery due to a rather dramatic winter snowstorm. When I was about halfway home, the traffic slowed and I realized there had been a major accident on the road. Cars were strewn all over the place. Some of the collisions looked serious, and emergency vehicles were just starting to arrive. It then dawned on me that if I had left when I had originally intended, I would have been in the middle of this mass of tangled cars and wreckage! I was stunned and somehow felt that that sense of a gentle hand on my shoulder had protected me that night. It was many years ago now and I still remember it vividly.

That experience comes to mind when I work with the dying and bereaved and they share the strength with which they feel the presence of a departed loved one around them. That hand on my shoulder felt tangible and real.

## The Bond with Our Pets

Animals and children are very sensitive to kinesthetic sensations, and sometimes a pet will respond to a presence in the room that is not felt or seen by others.

Michael lost his first wife to cancer. Her name was Ruth, and she had been a prominent opera singer in the coastal city in which they lived. She was admired for her beautiful voice and had a very large fan base. When it came time to have a memorial for her, he decided to invite a number of singers, musicians, and close friends to their home after the service for a more intimate gathering. It was a wonderful celebration for all; she had touched many lives with her gift of song.

After everyone left that evening and Michael had finished tidying up, he headed to bed with their little black poodle, Buddy, in tow.

Sometime around 2:00 a.m. he startled awake, realizing that Buddy had jumped down off the bed and gone downstairs. Sometimes he would have to let him out "to attend to his business" in the night, but curiously, this time Michael did not find the poodle waiting by the front door. Searching further, he went into the family room, which also had a door to the outside, but he wasn't there either. The only other door outside was up in the kitchen (the house was a split level), but when Michael arrived he still couldn't find Buddy. Wondering where his pet might have gone, Michael headed deeper into the kitchen area.

While standing beside the kitchen nook table, he suddenly spotted Buddy in the dining room. Their little dog was sitting in front of one of the empty dining room chairs. During his wife's memorial someone had turned the chair to position it facing out toward one of the large bay windows, with a view overlooking the ocean and distant islands.

What caught Michael's attention was that their dog was looking up at the chair as if someone was there. It must have been somebody that he knew well and loved, because his tail was wagging very rapidly, and his attention was so fixed that it was as if someone was talking to him.

Michael felt in that moment that Ruth had come back to say goodbye to their loyal four-legged family member, because of the sadness Buddy felt due to her not being around anymore. Buddy had been a close companion to Ruth, nestling in her bed for the last month of her life. Sitting in the kitchen watching Buddy for several minutes, Michael noticed that his tail, eventually, ever so slowly stopped wagging. The little dog then started looking around somewhat confused, as if Ruth had left but he didn't want her to go. Where had she gone?

Clearly Ruth's otherworldly presence had dissipated, and the dog finally gave up trying to find her. He then walked back into the kitchen and over to Michael, who picked the little one up in his big arms, held him close, and headed up the stairs and back to bed.

Later in the night, Buddy still didn't seem satisfied that Ruth was gone, and again he jumped down off the bed and ran downstairs to where the empty chair sat, searching for her. Michael followed him down and again waited patiently for him to come back to bed. This time, however, Buddy couldn't make contact. Once nestled back under the covers, both drifted back to sleep. For several days, Michael would notice his little dog returning to the chair throughout the day and looking up, hoping to see her. Never again did his tail wag in response to the presence he had experienced earlier.

From that day on, the dog stuck very closely to Michael until the little one himself died.

Buddy's companionship had been comforting to Michael after such a great loss. When Buddy had been in front of the chair on the evening of Ruth's memorial, it was an unexpected but truly touching moment for Michael, and it helped him come to terms with the loss of his wife in a heartfelt way. The bond of love between him and his wife was strong and lasting on so many levels.

## Perfume and Visits

Mary was unique in her creative expression and her awareness of the less tangible worlds. She had traveled the world and was a writer. Mary was lovable and very personable, and the medical staff became quite close to her when she was a patient on the palliative unit in the hospital. Due to challenging pain issues, she was on the palliative unit for many months. During that time, some of the staff read her books and were inspired by her philosophical approach to life. I also had the privilege of meeting her and found her life story intriguing. When she died, she was greatly missed.

Wearing products with a strong scent is discouraged around ill people because they are so sensitive, but Mary loved to wear a strong perfume. It was a recognizable and distinct fragrance.

As expected, closer to the time of her death she was sleeping more deeply due to her changing energy levels, and she could no longer engage in outer conversation. Mary was cocooning as the end of her life drew near.

Her sister, Kyla, loved her deeply. She was dedicated and kept vigil at Mary's bedside, but at one point Kyla was so tired she needed a break. That afternoon she headed back to her home to rest and have a shower. Unexpectedly, while Kyla was at home the strong scent of Mary's perfume, along with a tremendous sense of love, wrapped around her. It was so strong that Kyla wondered if Mary had come to let her know she had died.

Kyla thought she might get a phone call from the hospital, but it did not occur. She then decided to call the hospital to check in and found out that Mary was still alive. She had not died at that time, even though her presence and the smell of her perfume had been so strong that Kyla truly felt Mary had come for a visit.

Kyla later returned to the hospital and again sat vigil with great devotion. When I spoke to her, she said that the sense of love and gratitude that came with Mary's scent was so strong, she felt that she must have come to thank her for her support. Their bond of love was deep and lasting, and she remained at her sister's bedside until the day she died.

Mary was in the hospital for many months due to her pain management needs. Hers was not an easy case. During that time, Carol, the patient care coordinator on the palliative unit, had become quite fond of Mary. As a result, Carol had come to know Mary and her family more intimately than other patients with short-term stays. Mary was an interesting woman and had a range of colorful character traits that all the staff enjoyed. Her creativity, intuitive nature, and inspirational way of embracing life were gifts for all who met her. She died peacefully on the palliative care unit with her sister at her side.

A week after Mary's death, Carol was at the nurses' station attending to some routine tasks. As with Kyla's earlier experience, all of a sudden Carol felt Mary's presence near her, and just as quickly as she felt her presence, she too smelled Mary's perfume. It was strong and distinct. Later, Carol said it made her feel clearly as if the patient had come to say goodbye. She also felt her love and a sense of peace and gratitude when in the midst of the experience.

Both Kyla and Carol felt Mary's love, thanks, and support in unique ways. Both experienced her strong scent with the clear impression of her physical presence even though she was not physically in the room.

## Are You with Me?

Gordon, my former husband, died from a rare combination of three primary cancers in December of 2008. Normally a cancer has a main or primary site, and when the illness progresses it spreads by metastasizing to another area of the body. Gordon's case was unusual in that each cancer was unique, with varied characteristics, and each primary site was in a typical but different location. Each cancer was also reacting differently to the normal therapies, which made it challenging for the doctors who were involved in treating him. They discovered that the treatment protocol for one type of cancer could actually fuel the growth of the other types. Gordon had a severe reaction to one of the chemotherapies they prescribed. Decisions on the best way to proceed were challenging for all involved.

As the illness took greater hold, I took the four months leading up to his death off work to support him as he adapted to the myriad of health concerns. Prior to that time, he was in a mobile hospital bed at home, and friends were an incredible support, sitting beside with him in shifts throughout the day while I still had to maintain my full-time job in hospice. While he was at home, I was often up for a good portion of the night trying to settle him. The cancer then progressed deeper into his spinal column, at times threatening the spinal cord. Due to his severe pain management concerns, he ended up on the palliative care unit in the hospital near our home, one different from the location where I worked. This was not an easy death to partner.

About three weeks after he died, due to work commitments I had to return to my role as program director. The hospice society had been gracious and had held my position open while I took time off. I was still exhausted and was concerned about how I would traverse the range of strong emotions from moving back into the hospice setting on a daily basis after such a deep and intimate personal loss. Unlike those who go back to work after a death to escape their loss, I had death and grief in my face every day, at every turn. I had to be extremely careful around patients and families when my heart was still raw, so as not to impose my story onto theirs.

I loved my husband deeply and thus my grief was intense. I wanted to make sure to really listen to what my heart needed to fully mourn this loss, so that I could honor our love and the incredible lessons gained from such a challenging time.

Ironically, as hard as it was to go back to hospice work, in other ways it was a truly nurturing environment, because I was around people who understood and were not afraid of the subject. Much support came from my many work colleagues, for which I am grateful to this day.

Grief still came in waves. Some days were better than others.

On one particular day in the summer following his death, I was really struggling. There had been many complex and emotional situations with our patients and families at work, plus staff and volunteers would come to me as a sounding board with their challenging situations. Little did they know how, in the previous months, there were days when it was all I could do just to find the energy to get out of bed and go to work. At night I would often curl up alone under the covers watching romantic movies, so as to give my heart the freedom to mourn in my own quiet way. *Message in a Bottle* and *The Ghost and Mrs. Muir* (an old black-and-white film) were favorites. Both were about deep, lasting, and eternal love. Both spoke to me due to my husband's love of the sea from his brief time in the navy during his youth. The first is about a widower struggling to find footing after his wife's death. The second is about the prospect of unending love, a connection that continues with the spirit of the departed, surviving beyond physical death.

That summer evening particularly stands out. After arriving home from work, I was at the back door, exhausted and wondering if I really had the strength to continue in hospice work the way my heart was feeling. I was also missing my husband terribly. We had come to such an intimate place of loving before he died that there were times I felt as though my chest and heart were one invisible gaping wound due to his absence.

As I stood at the door, I dug into my purse trying to find my keys, fumbling to find the right one on the key chain. It seemed to elude me, and I was getting discouraged trying to find it. All of a sudden, I felt my husband as strongly as if he were standing right next to me. I knew his essence well, and it was as if he was not only standing next to me but wrapping his love around me with all his heart.

I stopped with keys in hand and just stood there in the rich sense of his company and love. Then I said inwardly, "Is that you, honey? Is that you?" It really felt like him.

Again, a strong wave of love wrapped around me, and again I sensed he was with me. I wondered if it was truly him, if he could still feel me, see me. How did this really work, now that he had died? Was he really able to connect with me after he had gone? His presence was distinct and palpable!

Eventually the sensation passed, and I managed to find the right key, open the door, and head inside. It wasn't an easy evening or next few days. Tears kept coming in private waves, and I felt very alone. I tried to nurture myself as best I could, to make it through the rest of the week. Weekends were my solace, and I often spent time out in nature, always a balm for my heart.

At that time I had a beautiful German shepherd named Angel. She was a graceful, gentle animal. She had been through her own health challenges but had stabilized and loved to go for walks with me.

On the weekend, I decided to take her to one of our favorite off-leash dog parks near the mountains. The trails wind through woods next to a rushing mountain stream and eventually up a mountainside, adding to the stunning images on the hike. It was a beautiful sunny day when Angel and I arrived at the park and started our walk together.

We crossed a pedestrian bridge over the river, and while we were walking along the upper part of the riverbank, Angel suddenly took off down a path she had never taken before, disappearing out of sight. I didn't want her to get lost, so I ran after her through the trees, down to the riverbank, eventually coming out at the riverside. I was really curious as to what was prompting her to go that way. She had never done that before.

The sun was glistening on the water that rushed over the rocks; the sound of the river was soothing. To my surprise, when I turned around in this little forest patch, right in front of me was a memorial altar for dogs that had passed away. I couldn't believe it. I had never seen it before! There were little urns, pictures, and notes scattered on a makeshift mantle. I was quite touched by the discovery; it was a magical surprise to find in this pristine patch in nature.

After taking in the heartfelt sentiments displayed before me, I looked up, and near the altar, on a tree, was pinned a piece of paper with writing on it. It seemed to almost call me over, as though the words were illuminated somehow.

The memorial altar had made me think of others who were grieving, and it touched on my own grief and feeling of being alone. Angel was content playing in the woods nearby, and so

I quietly walked over to read the piece of paper. When I got closer I could see it was a poem.

This was just days after feeling Gord's presence and asking, "Is that you, honey? Is that you?"

When I looked up and began to read the title and the words, tears welled up. I just wept, standing in front of the tree in the forest. His presence once again wrapped around me, and I could feel his love strongly.

Here is the poem that was pinned to the tree:

### It's Me

*I stood by your bed last night; I came to have a peep.*
*I could see that you were crying; you found it hard to sleep.*

*I whispered to you softly as you brushed away a tear.*
*It's me, I have not left you; I'm well, I'm fine and I am here.*

*I was close to you at breakfast, I watched you pour your tea.*
*You were thinking of the many times*
*your hands reached out to me.*

*I was with you at the shops today; your arms were getting sore.*
*I longed to take your parcels, I wished I could do more.*

*I was with you at my grave today; you tend it with such care.*
*I want to reassure you that I am not lying there.*

*I walked with you toward the house as you fumbled for your key.*
*I gently put my hand on you; I smiled and said, "It's me."*

*You looked so very tired and sank into a chair.*
*I tried so hard to let you know that I was standing there.*

*It's possible for me to be so near to you each day.*
*To say to you with certainty, "I never went away."*

*You sat there very quietly and then smiled; I think you knew ...*
*In the stillness of the evening, I was very close to you.*

*The day is over. I smiled and watched you yawning.*
*And said, "Good night, God Bless. I'll see you in the morning."*

*And when the time is right for you to cross the brief divide,*
*I'll rush across to greet you and we'll stand side by side.*

*I have so many things to show you. There is so much to see.*
*Be patient, live your journey out, then come home to be with me.*

Unknown Poet

# Chapter Six

# Dreams

*Our truest life is when we are in dreams awake.*
Thoreau

## Insights About Death and the Afterlife

Throughout history, the topic of dreams has been a mystery in itself. Covering lucid dreaming to the metaphoric symbols in dreams, many books have been written and much research done on the subject.

Dreams are a powerful source of insight before, during, and after a death. For the dying, they can be a way of working through fears or highlighting issues that are unresolved. Those who are dying can have dreams that indicate the exact time of death and give vivid insights into the journey ahead, causing greater peace and calm.

Loved ones who have passed on often come back to connect as companions or to offer heartfelt encouragement for the dying. Some of the dying have dreams that feel more like lucid out-of-body experiences, giving them a sense of identity outside of their mere physical shell, making it easier to let go of the body in death.

The bereaved also find dreams to be powerful in healing their grief. They too claim to have experiences of loved ones who have died returning to remind them that life continues on, that they are okay, and that love does not die.

A wealth of insight can come from the tapestry of dreams to offer greater ease in this time of transition. It is important to acknowledge the full range of experiences, from the lucid to the literal and the metaphoric.

# The Merry-Go-Round

Kathryn was one of the palliative patients in the hospice residence. She had a love for life that was infectious and she was an inspiration for all who engaged with her. She even started a group called the "Hospice Divas" during her stay and had T-shirts made up for the other female patients who became part of her special team. Kathryn told me a beautiful story of a dream her father had before he died of lung cancer years before. She was now facing her own mortality, dying of the same illness.

Kathryn had grown up in the Maritime provinces of Canada. Her father's family was very poor, so luxuries were not easily afforded. When he was a young boy, he was not able to go to the circus when it came to town because the family was struggling financially. He longed to get inside the fence and experience all the magical things that the circus offered. Since he could not afford the ticket, he would peek through the slats in the fairground fence, trying to catch a glimpse of the wonders at hand. Most specifically, he wanted to ride the merry-go-round. He longed for the experience as he watched others take delight in the ride. It became a symbol of something very magical for him, wrapped in childlike wonder.

Just days before he died, Kathryn's father had a dream that he shared with the family. He told them it had seemed like it was more than a dream—like a lucid, real experience. As he drifted off to sleep, he became aware of two light-filled angels flying toward his bed. They lifted him under his arms, out of his body, and took him up and up, through the sky, until they finally came to their destination. They flowed with grace and their love wrapped around him as they accompanied him on the journey.

When they arrived, he was thrilled to see a magnificent merry-go-round before them! His heart danced with joy and his childlike wonder instantly returned.

The angels invited him to take a ride and flew him over to settle him onto the saddle of one of the horses. His horse was stunning, exquisitely carved with an array of bright colors and a strong mane. The musical ride then began and he surrendered to the experience, relishing the sensation of the wind flowing through his hair while the horses were in motion. He was so happy. Laughter filled his heart and love wrapped around him.

The angels stayed with him the whole time, and when the ride was over, they once again lifted him up and carried him back down to where his physical body lay. Soon after, he awoke from the dream and felt a tremendous sense of peace. When he later shared the experience with his family, he said he knew where he was going and was no longer afraid to die. It was obvious to all that his outlook had changed dramatically. He died peacefully in his sleep a few days after he shared this with his children and family.

As Kathryn told me of her father's dream, I could see that it was bringing comfort to her now, as she faced her own mortality.

As she neared the final stages of her own life, her daughter told me that Kathryn kept repeating that she needed to get to the lighthouse. It was a fitting image, since she was from a coastal area of the country where lighthouses are designed to keep those at sea safe in stormy weather. They were strong symbols of Kathryn's home, her safety, and her family roots. Kathryn died with her family at her side, offering love, compassion, and encouragement. The light from the lighthouse was the beacon that came to guide her on the journey ahead.

## "You Can't Take Away This Fear"

To share a very powerful example of a dream experience, I must take you back to a moment with my former husband

Gordon, which occurred prior to his death. It had been weeks since he had been admitted to the palliative care unit at our local hospital. He was reaching that very tender turning point when it became clear to me that his physical death was inevitable. He had only months of life left, and the struggle to embrace every last bit of the time here intensified. Every day, I was reminded of the gift of time and how each moment with those we love is so precious.

His doctors were trying various palliative medications to attend to his discomfort. It was an incredibly vulnerable time for him and also for me as I tried to find a way to hold his suffering with grace and find meaning in it all.

When he was admitted into the hospital because he needed more extensive pain management and emotional reassurance, I took a leave of absence from work to be with him. I would stay at his bedside on the palliative unit during the day, sometimes heading home for a few hours' respite in the afternoon, or for a sleep at night, to attempt to find a way to rejuvenate. Though we had made the choice not to have children, I was like a mother bear protecting her cub. It was fascinating to me to see how strong my maternal instinct was, especially regarding the vulnerability, care, and well-being of someone I loved. I learned that often when the physical pain is managed, the deeper emotional and spiritual pain has space to surface more dramatically. Though the medical staff were happy when he was physically stable, they did not always see the deep emotional work that was taking place as a result. Gord was not one to show his emotions, but they surfaced in volcanic proportions as he was traversing his dramatic physical changes. Holding space for that took a lot of energy and love. My heart was grieving and suffering too.

I once read a beautiful quote from aviator Anne Morrow Lindbergh about her husband, the famous pilot who was the first to fly across the Atlantic. It was a reflection she had after his death. I have since searched for the original source and not been able to find it. But the way she expressed her marriage resonated with me. She said that being married to Lindbergh was like walking into a gale-force wind every day: it took every ounce of her strength. She also said that when he died, she realized that she not only missed the wind but that she had been transformed by it.

Gord was my gale-force wind, and through this time of struggle I referred to him that way. He was a survivor, passionate about life; he was not going to leave this world without a fight. He embraced life with determination and could be quite vocal about his opinions. This was especially true if someone ventured into topics around natural health care and the economy.

The theme of cancer was not foreign to Gordon. Sadly, he had watched his first wife die of cancer in her early fifties and they also lost a child, close to eight years old, to leukemia during their marriage. So, cancer stirred up very sensitive emotions for him around the medical system, general health care, and his own grief. It was not easy for him to trust the allopathic approach and medical doctors in general, which made it even more challenging for me.

Now he was facing his own cancer journey, and vulnerability was not his strong point. He was quite a few years older than me and clearly from a generation in which the qualities of tenacity and survival were key to his upbringing and way of being. That could be challenging, but I also loved that strength in him, which made me feel safe and protected. I don't believe I ever saw him afraid in all the years of our marriage; if he had been afraid, he concealed it well.

One morning as I walked through the door to his hospital room, I was disheartened to see this tall, six-foot-three man curled up in the fetal position with his head at the foot of the hospital bed. He was wearing one of the rather flimsy hospital gowns they provide and he had thrown off his covers. I had never seen him this way, and concern instantly overtook me. He looked like an infant, vulnerable and exposed.

I knew he was not doing well and quietly asked him what was going on. His high distress level was visible on his face— he seemed shaken to his core.

Gord told me that in the night he had had a terrible dream, more like a nightmare, but it had felt real. I gently asked him to tell me what had happened, shifting my attention to hold his fear with care. He said in the dream he was on a staircase, and as he was walking down the steps he could see that the stairs were broken off, falling away to pure darkness below. After the drop-off point, all that was left was nothingness. A powerful wave of fear had consumed him, because he knew if he let go he would fall endlessly into the dark cavern below. He had been frozen by the emotion and gripped the railings tightly so that he wouldn't tumble into an endless abyss.

Shortly after, he had woken up in a panic. The sensations of fear and falling were so real that he buzzed for the nurses to come help. He told me that when they arrived he desperately pleaded with them to tie his arms to the bed railings so he couldn't fall. Instead, the nurses gently calmed him and helped orient him to the room. They let him know that there was no threat to be concerned about, he was safe, and he had just had a bad dream.

As Gord shared the experience, he told me that he had never felt fear like that in all his life. It was strong and had overtaken him in a way he could still feel in his racing heartbeat. His body language reflected the intensity of his distress. He then looked at me from his curled fetal position in the hospital bed, pointing his finger and saying with determination, "You can't talk me out of this fear! You can't talk me out of this fear!"

I looked at him and in the most caring way possible said, "I know, but I can love you and be there for you. You will not be alone in this."

Then I went over and climbed into the hospital bed with him. Lying down behind him, I pulled him close to me and held him in my arms, wrapping my whole body around him with the utmost tenderness, much as a mother would when her infant has had a bad dream at night. I did everything I could to help him feel that my love was wrapping around him too, so that he felt nurtured and safe. I stroked his head and whispered loving sentiments to him to help calm his troubled heart. It was a breathtaking and tender moment, and I just stayed in the silence, holding him, loving him, feeling my heart beat next to his for the longest time. I was not trying to direct his feelings, rather just letting him be in the truth of what needed to surface and the deeper wisdom it was calling for.

After a time, his fear settled, his body calmed, and he sat up and turned around to crawl under the covers in the natural direction the bed was laid out. He put his head on the pillow and I tucked him in, wanting him to feel cozy and warm. I settled into a chair at his bedside, and it wasn't long before he fell asleep.

It was a turning point in the journey to his physical death. The metaphors in the dream were strong around his letting go into the unknown of what was to come. The pain had not been easy, which added to the uncertainty, but his heart started coming to terms, in a greater way, with his own dying. I knew the truth of that the minute he shared the dream. And he was right: I couldn't talk him out of the fear. His greatest need in that moment was my love and compassion, along with my support, to help him find his way and his own answers that would settle his heart on this journey. They needed to come from an organic place within him in order to be real and authentic.

As the weeks passed, his perceptions on the experience began to change, and then one day he happened upon a passage in a book with an inspirational theme that helped him hold his suffering in a different light. Somehow the words spoke to him in a way that gave meaning and purpose to all the pain that he had to endure in his physical and emotional bodies. He had now found a way to hold his suffering as a rich opportunity to grow, and he believed everything was in its right place. Through the pain he was being "broken open" and humbled to a new awareness of life and love. It was profound to watch. I too was being transformed, by companioning him through the transition.

Later I clearly remember asking him what he thought had caused that depth of fear. I said to him, "You are one of the most fearless people I know. You embrace life with an openness, curiosity, and passion, like very few people do. What was different this time to cause the fear?"

He looked at me and said, "Normally in life, you have a sense of what is to come, but this time I can't touch it, I can't see it, I can't feel it. I have to trust it in a way I have never had to trust before."

I listened silently and reflected on the depth of that truth.

We think we know how we will face death, but when we are standing on that cliff, about to jump off into a great unknown, how will we really feel in the moment? What will give us the courage we need to face this invisible unknown?

He did die peacefully months later, cradled in my arms as he took his last breath. He had come to a place of acceptance before his time of departure. He told me that it was my love that made the difference. In turn I watched as the physical challenges opened him to a greater vulnerability and love than I had seen in our whole twenty years together. He was transformed in stunning ways that in turn impacted and transformed my own heart.

## The Painter

Claire was the executive director for a hospice society. She shared with me this touching dream her father John had before he died.

John had been a house painter and decorator all his life. The swatches, with their vibrant range of colors, the creativity, the paint cans, and the brushes were central to his experience. At the age of eighty-six, he was taken by ambulance to the local hospital, and while there he was diagnosed with what turned out to be end-stage heart disease.

The family brought him home six days later at his request, and he died after only three days at home.

Claire said that the first day he was home, he asked her and her sister to sit down—he wanted to tell them about a dream he had had while he was in hospital. She said he related it in this way: "I was dying ... and I knew I was dying ... And it felt wonderful! It was peaceful, I wasn't afraid, and I was moving toward something that felt really good. Then I became aware that there were *others* with me, and one of these others—I could not see them but I could *sense* them—asked that I 'pick a color.' He said he picked yellow, and the instant message back was that 'it isn't the right color' and as a result 'it isn't time' for him. He remembered being very upset, because he really didn't want to come back, yet the next thing he knew, he was aware of being in his hospital bed."

Claire told me that when she related this story to a friend on the morning her dad died, she was in tears. Her friend then very gently said to her, "Well, Claire, it sounds to me like today your dad picked the 'right color.'" Claire said she couldn't help but laugh—it brought lightness to her grieving heart.

Later they found out that between the time her dad reluctantly came back from the dream and the time he died six days later, he and her brother had had an opportunity to come together and resolve their differences in a way that had not been possible previously. Claire and her sister have always wondered if his "coming back" gave the two men the time they needed to heal the conflict. There had been discord between them and they were able to resolve it. They would like to think the added time was given for this to occur.

## "I Am All Right"

When I was eighteen, I experienced the traumatic loss of someone I held dear: my closest girlfriend Susan died suddenly, unexpectedly, through a very tragic death. Her passing ripped into my heart and life and turned me upside down. The grief was beyond overwhelming. Life had instantly changed, and my innocent view of it was now dramatically challenged. Nothing made sense in the same way anymore. I felt out of sync with my peers and their objectives to move forward to the next level of academic pursuit at university.

I had a hard time concentrating on my studies, which is a normal grief response after such a loss. My grades plummeted, and that was a concern in my last qualifying year of high school. My family was at a loss to know what to do and how to support me. They too were devastated by the loss of this cherished young woman whom they loved so dearly. My mother was also very close to Susan's mother and was spending a lot of time in their family home in support of my friend's parents and brother as they came to terms with the news of her death.

High school ended. My grades had suffered, but I crawled to the finish line of my graduating year and surprisingly was accepted into my first year of university with the goal of a degree in marine biology. For most of my childhood I had wanted to be a doctor, but in the eleventh hour I changed my mind. Truth is, I wanted to take a year off to find the direction that felt right, not just pick something because it was deemed to be the "right" next step. However, my parents encouraged me to stay the expected academic route. My heart wasn't ready. Life had changed and what had felt concrete in the past no longer was reliable in the same way.

Marine biology seemed to be an interesting second choice, clearly less daunting than the years of additional study a medical career would ask of me, were I to embark on that. Ironically, later in my hospice work part of my duties were to attend various weekly medical rounds, and as a result I was immersed within the medical community. Many colleagues of mine are doctors and nurses.

Since childhood, I have loved water and its fluid nature: inviting and soothing, yet powerful. I became a lifeguard in my teen years and would spend hours in the pool immersing myself in the sensation of the water and the freedom it offered. Learning to flow with water, its movement and grace, parallels companioning the dying and navigating the varied currents of emotion and discovery that surface on their journey to death.

That fall I reluctantly left home for the university campus in another city, but it had only been six months since the death of my girlfriend, and instead of feeling stronger, I found my loss was gaining impact on my heart and my life's direction. The truth that Susan was never coming back took greater hold. I could barely focus on the work; I didn't want to be there. The scientific theories seemed harsh in the context of the journey I was engaged in. Literal concepts seemed to invade a heart that just wanted to be loved and heard in a compassionate way, a heart that just wanted the pain to go away. Theories about life paled in comparison to the raw truth of living it. Innocence had lost its footing.

I clearly remember one evening at my dorm desk, taking out a pencil and sketching a drawing. I drew a picture of a woman standing on a cliff, the strong wind ripping at her tattered coat. Her long dark hair was blowing violently in the wind. She stood alone, looking out over the ocean. The sun was setting. I pulled back after being totally immersed in creating the image and knew instantly the lone female was me. The sorrow and loneliness dripped off the page. Life did not hold the joy it once had. I struggled to find meaning in this loss.

After a poor academic beginning, I announced my decision to leave university after the first semester. This was difficult for my family. They tried to persuade me to stay, but I was no longer comfortable with the pressure to perform in an avenue I could not relate to in my grief. It does take a lot to have the courage to be different. I refused to take a path that didn't fit my authentic rhythm at the time. My friend's death brought that need to the fore. There would be challenging lessons for growth ahead. Many judged my decision unfairly, but I knew that an authentic path of discovery was the only way I could traverse this painful turning point. I honestly did not really know what that would mean. With grief's hold on my being, I couldn't fake enthusiasm.

Not long after, I remember consciously making a strong decision that I would *follow my heart*. I would let my heart be my guide in life. Even if the way I did things was a little less conventional, not necessarily the "right" way by society's standard, it would be the right way for me if I was to live an authentic life, one of honest purpose and meaning. That was a pivotal moment for me. Not an easy choice, but an important one.

Recently, my beautiful ninety-six-year-old father and I had a discussion about that choice. He was very honoring and said that he wished he had been that wise in his youth. It was an affirming moment for me.

After leaving university I moved back in with my parents to evaluate my next step in life. To keep busy I enrolled in some part-time courses at the local university, a curriculum different from the one I had left behind at the other school. Moving away from the sciences this time, I took courses in psychology and the arts, including one course in photography.

My mortality was in my face at a young age, and I was already starting to ask deeper questions of life and its meaning. No one was given permission to view Susan's body at the time of her death, due to the injuries to her physical body. This added to the challenge of accepting the reality that she was gone. Night after night for months on end, I had nightmares of searching for her, trying to find her with no success. They were exhausting dreams.

Finally, one night just a few months shy of the one-year anniversary of her death, I had a dream. But this dream was different. It was so lucid it felt like a real experience, and it was as life-changing as many proclaim a near-death experience to be.

The dream experience began within the theme of everyday events. It was set in my family home, and I was upstairs looking for a camera to do a project I had been assigned. As I came down the staircase, my eye caught a camera resting in someone's outstretched hands. I looked up and there was my girlfriend, Susan, holding the camera and standing in the vestibule by the front door!

I couldn't believe it. I had been looking everywhere for her, and there she was! But she looked different from her physical self. Yes, her facial appearance was the same, but she was radiant in a way that is hard to describe—it was as if she was filled with light. Her whole being was radiant. Emanating from her and extending outward was the most incredible aura of light, which danced with an array of different colors. She was glowing and her body was like a flowing gown of white brilliance.

Amazed to see her, I expressed my concern for her well-being: "Are you okay? I have been looking everywhere for you."

She then responded, "I came to let you know that I am all right. You have been worrying and I wanted to reassure you."

She began to walk from the vestibule, just inside the front door, through the living room and motioned for me to follow. I was so excited to see her, and in a rather enthusiastic and yet somewhat anxious manner, I started to ask again if she was all right. "Where are you?" All kinds of deeper questions were spilling from my mouth as I stumbled along behind her in awe.

She listened in silence as we walked, and then ever so gently she turned and extended her hand to me. When I took her hand, the most incredible thing happened. After many years, it is still hard to try to describe it in words, but I can remember it, and I still feel it as if it were happening now. This strong wave of pure love flowed from her hand to my hand, up my arm, and all the way through my body, like a waterfall of love that completely calmed all the anxiety I felt.

Every erratic emotion naturally settled, and my being felt as though it was enveloped in a sea of loving grace.

I was actually surprised by this and looked into her eyes. Without a word she just nodded, smiled in acknowledgement, and continued to guide me toward the dining room, holding my hand. Once at the dining room table, we pulled out two chairs and faced each other to have a chat. Again, I threw out my array of questions: "Are you okay? Where are you?" I was worried about her, due to the unexpected nature of her death.

She looked at me with the greatest of care and compassion and reassured me again. "I am indeed okay." She assured me that she was in the most amazing place and that there was tremendous love there. She also told me that she had met many new friends and was content, that I didn't need to worry about her well-being. She was very happy.

I asked her if she wanted me to be with her.

She said directly, "*No!* We will be together again one day, but not now."

In fact, she made an interesting statement. She said, "We are not normally allowed to do this, but since you were so distressed, I was given permission to see you."

We talked a while longer, and then the most incredible thing happened. The window in the room was slightly different in the dream experience, more like a big picture window. It burst open with an incredible force of light and sound. The most brilliant white light came pulsating in through the open window. It was so bright that when I tried to look in that direction I almost felt blinded, and I had to squint my eyes due to its intensity. Along with the light was a deep sound, like an electrical hum, pulsating in, penetrating my chest and heart center. It was like the feeling you experience when a speaker is turned up high and you feel the bass vibration deep in your chest.

Both the light and sound were powerful beyond measure, beyond anything I recall having known before that moment.

For lack of a better way of expressing it, it felt like God (or something greater in expression) was calling her.

I turned to look at her and she quietly said, "I have to go now."

I said, "I know."

It was apparent that she needed to return to wherever she had come from. She looked at me one last time with the utmost compassion in her eyes and said, "Are you all right now?"

I said, "Yes."

The next thing I was aware of was waking up to the sunniest of mornings. The experience was so powerful, so real. On some level it felt like I had actually been with her, talking to her.

It was also so impactful that I could hardly move. I just wanted to stay in the essence of what had taken place. Also a knowing within me was strong. This was not an intellectual knowing but a rich sense in my heart that I was now aware of two things—that she truly was okay and that, at least for me, there was no doubt that there was life after death. I was waking up that morning with my being knowing in a different way the truth that there is life after death, beyond an intellectual concept or rendering. I find it very difficult to explain or find accurate words to share this sincerely with another.

This experience transformed my grief and my inability to go forward. The light in the experience was brilliant, but the sound had reached into my heart and lifted my grief in a way no grief counselor could possibly have done. That alone was fascinating.

Even though my grief was not totally gone, I was able to go forward with greater ease because it had been transformed in a way that made her death and my life more bearable.

This lucid dream experience also changed the course of my life. Questions about dreams, about the less tangible elements at play in life, and about our purpose for being here became big parts of my focus. I began a much deeper spiritual search for answers and meaning to this life at the age of eighteen.

# Chapter Seven

# Love and Compassion

*Where there is love there is life.*
Gandhi

## At the Heart of Living and Dying

Our society puts so much emphasis on the power of the mind, yet we are less inclined to honor another very powerful source of insight—the heart. Research from the Institute of Heart Math in California suggests that the heart is an intelligence center in constant communication with the brain and in turn the rest of the body. As we know, negative emotions and stress can have tremendous impact on the heart's natural rhythms, health, and well-being.

When I train hospice volunteers and staff to sit quietly in support of the dying and bereaved, I encourage them to notice when they are in their heads versus being in their hearts. Each alignment, head or heart, has its own unique expression and rhythm that other people can distinctly sense.

One of the greatest dances at the end of life is the dance between love and fear. Throughout history, love has been perceived as being aligned with the heart; fear often comes from our thoughts and beliefs and is therefore considered to be aligned with the head. Love expressed in the form of deep, empathetic listening bridges to a place that opens the heart. When fear is present in the dying or their loved ones, a companion's love and compassionate presence is more powerful than words. In the silence alone, when love is present, profound transformations happen. To listen without judgment, giving space to all that is occurring, may be the greatest gift anyone can give to another human being.

Our common language truly is love and compassion. The tender language of love creates a sense of safety and trust during the most vulnerable times of change. Love supports the dying person to surrender more naturally into the end of their life.

We all are born, attempt to find love, find love (or not), and eventually die. The individuals we support in hospice care are from a range of faith backgrounds and cultures. Exploring the power of love aids in a more peaceful passing by helping to overcome fear, transcend our differences, and speak to our shared humanity during the universal life experience of dying.

Hospice volunteers sit alone with dying patients in vigil during the last hours of life. The love they feel in the silence is strong and tangible. It is as if the air in the room takes on a different tone. Being with the dying changes hospice workers in ways they often cannot put into words, but they feel privileged to be invited into observing and being present for this sacred transition.

## What Makes Your Heart Dance?

There are people who come into our lives at different times, who touch us in ways we could never have imagined. Sam was such an individual. He was in his early seventies when I met him on the palliative unit for the first time. The ravages of his illness were definitely apparent. He had lost a great deal of weight and his physique was frail and emaciated. The housecoat he wore seemed as though it belonged to someone else; it hung loosely on a frame that had once housed much greater physical strength and bulk.

The nurses said that he was an extremely private man. He had never married, and he did not accept visitors easily. In fact he could be quite gruff at times if he felt intruded upon.

Others had tried to approach him, but the conversations were often brief and many of the hospice volunteers were not comfortable visiting after the cool reception that ensued. They concluded that he preferred to be alone.

Watching Sam in the hall one day, I finally decided to say hello. As I approached, he appeared to have a lot on his mind, and his response to my greeting was not overly warm but rather cold, distant, and uncaring. No doubt he was battling a range of emotions as his body went through the changes that were occurring from the illness—not easy for anyone, let alone a man used to relying on himself. I didn't want to impose on his privacy and so I left him alone, but there was something about him that drew me in and made me wonder about his life experience.

I asked others if they knew how he had lived his life, and some of the nursing staff and volunteers shared that Sam had been a pilot. This theme had been at the center of Sam's life. He had flown planes in WWII. After leaving the military, he flew helicopters professionally, often in remote areas. A curiosity about the sky had woven into my life a number of times, due to my father's love of flying in my youth. I had never flown in a helicopter at the time and was intrigued about the prospect. I thought, if the moment presents itself, I will talk to Sam about flying.

As fate would have it, that opportunity arose while I was visiting Bill, the patient sharing Sam's room. After a nice discussion with Bill, while passing Sam's bed to leave I mentioned to him that I had heard he was a helicopter pilot. I began to share some funny stories about my father, who, with four daughters, tried to entice one of us to take up flying. Sam's mood lightened for the first time and he took delight in hearing the stories. I mentioned that the prospect of flying a helicopter was an interesting one and asked him how the propeller worked, comparing its action to the way maple seeds spiral down on the air currents. He laughed as I used this analogy but agreed that it was a good comparison. I was not a pilot at the time and was less versed in the mechanics of airplanes. The other patient, Bill, had become quite close to Sam while sharing the room. The three of us had a wonderful conversation that day and a quiet bond of trust began to form. The similar symbols of the helicopter and the maple seed were strong in my first meeting and connection with this man.

As I visited with Sam over the weeks, a sense of familiarity deepened. It was enjoyable, learning of his life and adventures in the sky; however, he was an incredibly private man, very much a loner. He had few close friends, no surviving family that came to visit, and had never married. Later I was glad to meet his close and very caring friends, Marianne and Joe, a couple who had arrived from out of town. Their bond of love with Sam was strong and they stayed for the final weeks leading up to his death. Marianne put her whole heart into caring for him, which helped Sam tremendously.

My connection with Sam grew to be very special. The nurses would joke that he had fallen in love with me, because they said he insisted on shaving every time he knew I was due to visit. This included the final weeks before his death, when his body had deteriorated to that of a mere skeleton. It touched me to hear that our time together brought some joy to his final days.

As I came to know Sam better, I realized he had a greater fear of death than I had initially perceived. He was now finally sharing with his closest friends pieces of the horrors he had experienced in WWII. At one point his plane was shot down and he endured horrendous and painful circumstances just to survive. He even hinted that he had been exposed to one of the "death marches" through foreign, grueling winter conditions. People who had known him for forty years later told me that they had never known of the challenges he had once faced, because he had kept them secret, buried within. No doubt his heart had experienced a lot of atrocities during that time, and knowing this helped me to understand his solitary nature. Unfortunately, over time these buried secrets had caused his heart to close to many people and aspects of life. He had become tougher to survive. He did not allow himself to become vulnerable or let many people become close.

It has been my observation that not everyone finds comforting ways to hold pain and suffering after witnessing such extremes, and my compassion for him, for all that he had endured, deepened.

As a result of his life experiences, Sam became a professed atheist. This became very clear when I walked into his room one day about a week before he died. He was sitting alone on the edge of his bed, shoulders and body slumped over in deep thought. He had become very close to his roommate, Bill, who had died only days before, and the bed was now deafeningly empty. Sam was clearly feeling the impact of that loss and in turn facing his own mortality with greater honesty. It was obvious by his expression and posture that he was burdened with something, but I didn't know what it was. Sitting there, he looked so frail—virtually just skin covering his emaciated shell.

Gently, I sat down next to him on the bed and put my hand on his shoulder. "It looks like you have a great deal on your mind today," I said. "Is there anything you would like to share?"

He did not respond right away and for the longest time sat looking down at the floor. Then turning to look at me with uncertainty in his eyes, he said, "I don't know if I can believe in God, so I am not sure what to focus on in this moment."

I held his question in silence for a moment, then smiling and with great enthusiasm asked him this question: "Is there anyone or anything that, when you think about that person or thing, it makes your heart dance? When you focus on that person or that thing, it makes your chest just want to explode with love?" My body language was quite animated when I offered the question for him to ponder.

At first, he just stared at me and then began to laugh, obviously not expecting my response. With a big smile he said, "Figures you would say something like that!"

Still sitting on the hospital bed, he looked down toward the floor and again, for the longest time, as if taking in my question, he seriously reflected on his answer. The silence was rich with reflection in that moment. Ever so slowly a smile came over his face and I could see his countenance begin to change. He turned to look at me and said quietly, "My dog. My dog makes me feel that way."

"Your dog," I said with a smile, acknowledging the unconditional love that animals so often provide.

Another silent pause took over as he continued to reflect on the question and look back down at the floor. This time the question seemed to move deeper into his being as he contemplated his answer. All of a sudden, as if a wave moved through him from his feet to the top of his head, lightness seemed to overtake him. His body language changed, he sat taller, and then he turned and looked at me to say, "But what really makes me feel that way is nature. The incredible peace I feel in the presence and beauty of nature." It seemed like an epiphanic moment for him.

Smiling back at him and looking him deep in the eyes, I said, "Then that is what you need to focus on, for it is the love in your heart that will help you make the transition. Focus on that love, those things that bring you joy. Surround yourself with those images."

We then had a special discussion about the precious moments he had had as a pilot in the solitude of nature. The peace he felt with the animals and the moments in which he observed the stunning colors of the sunsets and sunrises. He reminisced about breathing the crisp fresh air and smelling the rich scents in the forests.

Outside his window was a breathtaking view of a snowcapped mountain. Sam and I both agreed that the mountain symbolized something very sacred through its majesty and presence alone. We spoke of what a gift it was to have this beautiful mountain to view close at hand and about the power of the symbols of things dear to us that open our hearts. Sam seemed comforted and in good spirits when I left his room.

His dying process took greater hold in the days to follow and he became increasingly frail. He no longer had even the strength to shave for my visits, which he apologized for. He was a proud man, and I knew he was feeling self-conscious about the dramatic change in his physical appearance.

He told me that he thought he must be terrible to look at, but I responded by telling him that I thought he was beautiful just the way he was and I would take him any way he came. He laughed at my comment and again said it figured I would answer that way, always so positive.

I meant what I said.

There is an old saying: "The eyes are the windows to the soul." This reality becomes even more pronounced around the time of death, when the physical body loses its vibrancy but the eyes maintain light and a rich expression of life. The sparkle in his eyes was always welcoming and a precious reflection of the essence of the person I had come to know.

Days before his death, Sam told me he was trying to die but he didn't know how. Did I have any hints? Together, we created a visualization that included many of the precious images we had previously discussed, and coupled with that, he reflected on the music that he loved and that soothed him. Once again, I reminded him to focus on the love and peace he felt in nature, the image of the beautiful mountain outside his window in all its radiance, and the light it reflected. This visualization gently helped him to drift off to sleep.

My last visit with Sam was brief, as he was weak and couldn't talk, propped up by pillows in his bed to help his labored breathing. As I stood next to the bed, he slowly opened his eyes, which were beautiful, bright, and blue. My heart strings were certainly pulled as I looked into his eyes for what I sensed would be the last time. It was clear he was exhausted, and after a moment of silence I encouraged him to rest, for I wouldn't be staying long. He closed his eyes softly and a part of me felt torn. I didn't want to leave, but I knew it was time. I gently kissed him on the forehead, saying a final goodbye. The nurses let me know that he died peacefully the next day.

The metaphors of life are fascinating.

The day after his death I had to go into town for an appointment. On my drive home, I was thinking of Sam, and out of the corner of my eye I saw a car approaching from one of the on-ramps with a trailer in tow. To my surprise, sitting on the trailer was a helicopter! As I looked more closely I could see that it was actually the "shell" of a helicopter; the "guts" of the aircraft were gone. I marveled at the orchestration of that image in front of me! I had never seen that before—a mere empty shell of a helicopter being transported.

A smile came to my face.

The helicopter reminded me of Sam and the fact that when the energy of the person leaves at the time of death, the empty shell of a body is left behind. This image is similar to the metaphor of the butterfly shedding its cocoon and moving on. Each person will have a different perspective on what happens at this time of transition.

Though Sam was a declared atheist, nature was his solace; it brought great joy and love to his heart. When celebrated, those images helped him to make his transition from this physical life a peaceful one. Love and compassionate presence helped to settle his fear and supported him to embrace the journey at hand.

## Celebrating Our Humanity

While working as the program director for a hospice society in a very diverse city, I was privileged to meet people from many different countries, cultures, and faiths. My staff members and hospice volunteers could speak many languages, and I learned so much from each of them. Often when I listen to the conflict in the news between people of different religious backgrounds, I wish I could just bring them to a hospice or palliative unit for a day to see how our humanity can truly unite us rather than divide us.

Divjot was one of our long-time hospice volunteers. She is of South Asian and Sikh descent, and in many ways she considers herself spiritual in religious alignment. She is a loving and compassionate human being, and her presence on the hospital unit is calming not only to patients and family members but also to palliative care staff.

It was Good Friday and Divjot was working on the palliative care unit during her regular weekly shift, when she was approached by one of the nurses with a rather unique request. She was told that a family was in great distress and was asking if someone could offer prayer for their loved one. The patient they were referring to was an elderly woman on the unit who was being prepped for a surgical procedure and was terrified of going into the operation without a blessing. The family was doing everything to try to comfort her. The patient was already dealing with a life-limiting diagnosis and the thought of surgery in this weakened state was adding to her fear. Her family had asked for a priest to come and give a blessing, but no one was available to come to the hospital at that time, due to other commitments during the Easter holiday.

The nurse knew that Divjot was deeply spiritual, so she wondered if she would meet with the family to say a prayer for the woman. Divjot said she wanted to help the family, but she was a little concerned about whether she was equipped to give them what they needed, since she was not of the Christian faith. When she expressed this, the nurse reassured her that this was not an issue for the family—she had already given them this information. Though she was still somewhat reluctant, Divjot finally agreed to meet the patient and family. She did not know what she was going to say, but chose to trust that the moment would offer up the words that the woman and her family needed to hear.

Divjot is so filled with grace that I am sure the nurse had let the family know that she would speak from a loving and heartfelt place.

Prior to heading to the palliative unit that day for her volunteer shift, Divjot had done her own meditation. During that quiet time, she had offered herself and her life in whatever way she could best be of service to others. Life was now providing that opportunity.

Divjot is slight in build and quite graceful. When she walked to the nurses' station to meet the family, she noticed some of the men were quite large and muscular in build. They towered over her, which was initially intimidating, until they expressed their deep gratitude and welcomed her presence with open arms. They then led her into their mother's hospital room to be introduced. Divjot could immediately see that the woman was anxious, and offered loving words to help reassure her. As she stood by the woman's bedside, with her sons, daughters-in-law, and grandchildren filling the room, the words came gently and easily. When she began the blessing, she centered in her heart, closed her eyes, raised her hands in prayer, and then asked God to be with the woman to help her through the surgery. The prayer she spoke was simple, but it was a genuine expression of her faith in a loving God, a faith she believed she shared with the family despite the differences in religious affiliation. In her prayer she also included the doctors and nurses who would be doing the surgery and asked that their work be blessed.

Once she finished the blessing, there was initially silence in the room. Everyone was moved by her grace and sincerity. The family then thanked her for the blessing and the obvious comfort that the prayer brought to their mother. The tension broken, they all hugged, and she silently thanked them for the gift of knowing that, in those few moments of prayer, they were united in peace, compassion, and love. In the presence of their mutual faith in a universal divine power, they were not separated by religion, race, ethnicity, culture, age, gender, or class. Divjot says she herself was transformed by the experience, and it will stand out as one of the most memorable in her many years of hospice work.

## The Essence of Love

There is one moment that stands out in the midst of the challenging times when Gordon was at home dealing with the terminal illness that plagued his body. I will never forget that moment. It occurred one day during that early morning hour when the light is just starting to peek through the lingering darkness and when waking from sleep often brings greater wisdom and insight from a much broader realm of awareness.

Gord awoke and carefully sat up on the edge of the bed. Due to my concern for his pain, all my protective instincts were on high alert, which caused me to wake as soon as I heard him move. I instantly got out of bed and came around, standing in front of him, asking if he was all right. "Do you need more pain medication?"

He was looking down at the floor and did not respond to my inquiry right away. A few moments passed and then, shaking his head back and forth, still looking down in deep reflection, he said, "It is not about power and struggle at all. It is not about power and struggle."

This was not the response I was expecting, but it seemed to be coming from an authentic place within him. I wanted to engage in dialogue and responded by asking, "It is about love?"

Instantly, I could feel my words imposing themselves on the much greater experience he was immersed in. My mind was trying to define this epiphanic moment with words for him, but they fell short when I spoke them aloud. Rather, they were like a tremendous imposition and foreign to the truth of what he was actually experiencing.

He was silent and looked down for the longest time. I knew he was searching, with every ounce of his being, trying to find the words to respond, but the insights were far beyond the literal.

After a time, he quietly said, "It is about *the essence of love*, the *essence of love*. We make it so difficult, but it is so simple."

I was moved deeply by his reflection and knew that any other attempt at conversation or to define this moment would in a way be a violation of a profound spiritual realization he was engaged in, far beyond the mere parameters of a defined reality.

He was catching the truth of love in a much greater way, no longer a mere mental concept. I was being invited into it simply in the silence of the moment. Moving closer to him, with no words, I just held him. We stayed in a deep embrace for the longest time. It was a rich experience far beyond words, the silence textured.

# Epilogue

*If a man does not keep pace with his companions,*
*perhaps it is because he hears a different drummer.*
*Let him step to the music which he hears,*
*however measured or far away.*

Thoreau

## What Death Teaches Us
## About Life and Beyond

There are dimensions to life that clearly fall into the realm of mystery. When one is facing physical death, deep transitions highlight this truth and illuminate many unanswered questions about our very existence. How can we possibly not take the time to be present and learn from the subtle wisdom expressed during the physical dying process?

Over the years I have watched when people lose someone close and then their hearts start to shut down. The pain of grief is so deep that they quietly retreat from life or the prospect of loving again. Or they do things to escape from life so as not to feel too deeply again.

I didn't want that to happen to me. My father is ninety-six years old, and despite all that he has been through, including memories from his time in the British navy during WWII, he is an incredible example of someone who has kept his heart open to life. He is still curious about so many things. With great devotion, he loved my mother through a progression of Alzheimer's that lasted over ten years until her death. I am blessed to call him my father.

One day, months after Gord had passed, I clearly remember feeling my heart wanting to start to guard, to protect, to quietly shut down, as the pain of my loss was too

91

much. I was concerned. It has always been a goal of mine to keep my heart open to life, love, God, the Divine, and the greater mysteries of life. The individuals whom I have observed in my hospice work who have kept their hearts open to love and life almost always have richer experiences and relationships as a result.

So I took these reflections inside, deep into contemplation, which is what I do when I am unsure. I asked inwardly, "Show me what to do to keep my heart open to life. Show me how to keep my heart alive to love and life and continue to be childlike in how I approach things. What can I do to have the excitement of a child and be open to life as though it were new?"

As I was holding this reflection carefully in contemplation, ever so gently but distinctly an answer came: *gliding.*

"Gliding?" I protested out loud. "Are you kidding me? Here I am, grieving, and your answer is *gliding?"*

For those of you who aren't aware, gliding is flying a plane with no engine. Yes, a full-out plane, with cockpit and instruments but *no* engine. You are towed up by a power plane and released at a high altitude, learning to soar on the wind currents like an eagle. I had seen gliders in my youth when my father's interest in flying drew me in, though he himself flew planes with engines—never a glider!

I even tried an introductory flight in a Cessna when I was in my twenties, but I didn't like the noise of the motor and so didn't pursue lessons after that. In 1995, my husband and I both did an introductory flight in a glider with a pilot around the stunning mountains of British Columbia. When the tow plane released the plane for the first time and flew off, the glider slowed and was caught by the wind currents. I clearly remember the feeling: it was so profound for me, it brought tears to my eyes. It was like resting in the arms of God. It was so magical that I can't begin to describe the feeling. Stunning mountains all around and river valleys below, cradled only by the invisible wind currents.

Gord enjoyed the experience too, but he wasn't interested in proceeding beyond the initial experience at the time. Now here I was, fifteen years later, in contemplation, asking how to keep my heart open to life like a child in the midst of this grief, and the answer that came was *gliding.* I hadn't really thought of that in years, but the prompting was so strong I couldn't let it go. I called a few friends and within a week arranged for another introductory flight out at the airfield.

Despite my enthusiasm and the encouragement from those close to me to share the experience with them, I remember being exhausted on the day I had to make the long hour-and-a-half drive to the gliding club. Later, when standing on the grass airstrip and looking at the stunning mountains all around and this crazy plane with no engine in front of me, my thoughts reeled. "What in the world am I doing here? This is ridiculous. Maybe I heard wrong. I can't do this. I just want to go home!"

Not more than a heartbeat of a moment had gone by, when I looked up and saw walking toward me one of the older pilots, whom I had not met before. He reached out his hand and introduced himself as Harald. Ironically, there is someone in my life who has taught me so much spiritually—a cherished teacher—and his name just happens to be Harold. So when Harald introduced himself, I instantly paid attention.

He then leapt right into his presentation, and without hesitation, he said, "Life is a *three*-dimensional experience. Most people live life in a *two*-dimensional way, but life is a *three*-dimensional experience. If you take up flying, your whole perspective on life will change. When you see a tree and leaves, you won't just see a tree and leaves. When the leaves are turned in the opposite direction, you will see the wind. And you won't just see the wind, you will then see systems. And you won't just see systems, you will see how they interact with nature. If you take up flying, your whole perspective on life will change."

I couldn't believe his words. They were poetic in the moment, in how they spoke to my heart and my questions about life. It was because of his encouragement that I went forward and took up flying seriously. It has been an amazing experience to heal and embrace life again. It has caused me to look at many things in a different light. It is so beautiful to dance with the clouds high in the sky. Life looks different from that expansive bird's-eye viewpoint.

The metaphor of flying a glider and its parallels to the many dimensions of life is quite profound. There are the detailed components that are at play when handling the plane and strategizing for a safe flight. But there are also the less tangible components in nature that cannot be predicted and yet cause the experience to be more interesting. One must flow with the wind and nature's elements at play in the midst of the adventure—trust is a key factor. I have faced myself and many fears while up in the sky flying a plane with no engine, and I have become a stronger person for it.

Much like those facing their physical death, there is so much at play in life itself that we cannot see or formally define. The more we stay open to learn from all that they share, the more we will learn about this vast uncharted territory. In turn we can support each other more fully through this fascinating life transition. Discoveries regarding the rich dimensions and mystery of life are unending. Compassionate presence, love, and understanding are key during this sacred time.

How can we all better honor the mystery at the end of life, support our shared humanity, and in turn celebrate life to the fullest?

# Acknowledgments

First, I would like to thank the thousands of people whom I have had the privilege to support and work with during my many years in the hospice field. The stories from patients, their families, and colleagues make up this book. I am grateful they allowed me to share their experiences. Each person whom I have met has taught me a great deal in their own unique way about life and love.

Thank you to Andrew for his patience and love. You have been an incredible sounding board and support for both the book and the launch of my new education business. Your hours of help with computer issues and maintaining the integrity of this work have been invaluable. I am truly grateful for all you have brought into my life.

Tremendous gratitude is extended to Sri Harold for being such an amazing spiritual teacher and an example of love and compassion in my life and within the world.

To Nina Shoroplova, my editor, for being supportive and respectful of my voice yet thorough with her advice. To Geoff Affleck, for being a wonderful mentor and support while creating and launching this book. This is a big accomplishment for a first-time author, especially after being turned down by so many publishing houses previously.

Thanks to my sisters, Kathryn, Carol, and Heather, who have been a constant source of support and encouragement. Your kindness and love have helped when I have doubted the reason for even putting this out into the world. My dear friends Claire and Stuart, Evelin and James, Penny and Howard, Andrea and Mike, and Ingrid again for the unending encouragement and love; you are the definition of true friends. Linda Anderson for her love, friendship, initial editing, and creative support around this work. To Peter, Jack, Yves, John T., Dan S., Mike S., Ted, and Nick, for your belief in these stories and your quiet support.

To my palliative doctor friends and colleagues, Shikha and Aleco and Ruth, CNS, for your constant encouragement of this creative venture and your support for sharing my own unique voice to help others. Also for your acknowledgment of how powerful simple stories can be to help inform, inspire, and heal others.

To Jake, who loved these stories and continued to encourage me to share them with the world until he died. Your example of holding integrity around the art of storytelling within the medium of film will always stay with me.

To my former husband, Gordon, for all you taught me about deeper commitment and love. There are countless others who have helped over the years, but it would be too hard to capture all of them here. For all those people I offer my sincerest gratitude.

# Biography

Barbara Morningstar began serving in the hospice field over twenty years ago. During that time she worked on staff at three different hospice societies within the province of British Columbia, Canada. The most notable was at a hospice society where she held the position of program director for twelve and a half years. While there, Barbara oversaw their palliative and bereavement programs, counseling staff, and hospice volunteers. Her teams worked with palliative patients and their loved ones in the twenty-bed hospice residence, the eleven-bed Tertiary Palliative Care unit in the local hospital, and with people who were being supported to die at home in the community. The hospice also provided one-to-one grief support and grief groups to bereaved of all ages.

Over her many years in the hospice field, Barbara has supported thousands of people during this tender life transition. Her husband of twenty years died of cancer in 2008. She founded *In Autumn's Cocoon Education* in the fall of 2017 and is a key note speaker at major hospice and palliative conferences.

Barbara is presently offering her skills and years of experience in end-of-life care as an educator in the form of talks, workshops, and writing. More information can be found on her web site: www.inautumnscocoon.com. She would love to hear your stories of mystery, love, and healing around end-of-life transitions.

Made in the USA
Monee, IL
05 December 2020